SOLA SCRIPTURA DOESN'T *WORK*

25 PRACTICAL REASONS TO REJECT THE DOCTRINE OF 'BIBLE ALONE'

BY JOEL S. PETERS

Published by Catholic Answers, Inc.
2020 Gillespie Way
El Cajon, California 92020
1-888-291-8000 orders
619-387-0042 fax
catholic.com

Printed in the United States of America

Cover design by ebooklaunch.com
Interior design by Maria Bowman

978-1-68357-356-2
978-1-68357-357-9 Kindle
978-1-68357-358-6 ePub

To my Maria.

CONTENTS

ACKNOWLEDGMENTS

I am indebted to many students and colleagues at St. Joseph Regional H.S. over the years, to some very dedicated people at Our Lady of Perpetual Help Church, and to some very close friends, all of whom have motivated me to pursue excellence in the knowledge of our shared Catholic faith. They are too numerous to mention here, and I fear that I might overlook someone! I am truly grateful to all of them for having deeply enriched my life journey and faith formation as fellow sojourners on their way to heaven.

I am also grateful to Todd and Drew, who were instrumental in taking a rough stone and helping me to shape it into a polished gem. Their insights and suggestions were invaluable.

INTRODUCTION

There are many reasons why the Protestant doctrine of *sola scriptura* is false. And there are many fine books written by Catholic apologists that show its deficiencies from a scriptural perspective, and that soundly refute the standard proof texts Protestants use to defend it.

I want to take a different approach.

I want to show how *sola scriptura* fails not only according to the Bible, but according to other kinds of tests—practical, logical, and historical. By every measure, the doctrine of *sola scriptura* falls apart, and so we must reject it as not being part of "the faith that was once for all delivered to the saints" (Jude 1:3).

Practical: Does *sola scriptura* actually work? Does it provide useful, needed guidance on and clarity to Christian doctrine, worship, and behavior? Are the necessary structures in place for it to be used in a meaningful and accessible way?

LOGICAL: Does *sola scriptura* make sense? Is it intrinsically coherent, or does it lead to fundamental contradictions and inconsistencies?

HISTORICAL: Did *sola scriptura* exist throughout the Church's history? Was it part of the deposit of faith given by Christ to the apostles and therefore used by the Church as the rule of faith from the first century to the present day? Is there clear evidence of this?

I have also included throughout the book a series of *Questions to Ask*. Their purpose is twofold: to test the veracity of *sola scriptura* on the basis of each reason given and to invite further honest discussion.

Let me go on record at the start: I firmly believe that my Protestant brothers and sisters love the Lord Jesus and earnestly strive to be faithful to him. I also want to affirm the high regard they have for the scriptures, acknowledging them to be what they truly are: God's words to humanity. I choose to believe that when Protestants rail against the Catholic Church and accuse it of adding to God's word, they do so with a sincere conviction that the scriptures must remain inviolate and must hold the place of highest regard in the Church.

Catholics share this conviction; the Church has been venerating and safeguarding the scriptures for many centuries. After all, its members wrote the New Testament. As the Second Vatican Council put it,

> the Church has always venerated the scriptures just as it venerates the body of the Lord, since, especially in sacred liturgy, it unceasingly receives and offers to the faithful the bread of life from the table both of

> God's word and of Christ's body. It has always maintained them, and continues to do so, together with Sacred Tradition, as the supreme rule of faith, since, as inspired by God and committed once and for all to writing, they impart the Word of God himself without change, and make the voice of the Holy Spirit resound in the words of the prophets and apostles.
>
> Therefore, like the Christian religion itself, all the preaching of the Church must be nourished and regulated by Sacred Scripture. For in the sacred books, the Father who is in heaven meets his children with great love and speaks with them; and the force and power in the Word of God is so great that it stands as the support and energy of the Church, the strength of faith for its sons, the food of the soul, the pure and everlasting source of spiritual life (*Dei Verbum* 21).

Although I admire Protestants for their zeal for God's written word, at the same time, I must point out charitably but candidly that, in their zeal, Protestants have created a doctrine that divorces the scriptures from their historical and ecclesial contexts, creating an unprecedented doctrinal rupture.* Five hundred years later, Christianity is still reeling.

Protestants and Catholics are not as separated as they once were. Tempers have cooled since the volatile events of the sixteenth century, and Protestants and Catholics have made

* Though the Eastern Orthodox churches broke away from unity with Rome in the eleventh century, that rupture did not center on the question of whether the scriptures serve as the believer's sole authority. Hence, the doctrine of *sola scriptura* was effectively a novelty well into the second millennium: even though John Wycliffe introduced the idea in the fourteenth century, it did not become widespread until the sixteenth, with Martin Luther.

some progress in identifying common ground.[3] Although important differences still exist, a spirit of mutual respect, understanding, and conciliation seems to be growing. And so, without minimizing or overlooking the theological issues that still separate us, we can acknowledge the need to direct our efforts to creating and sustaining the unity that Jesus desires for his Church.

One of those remaining issues centers on the Bible. Protestants assert that the Bible is the believer's only infallible rule of faith, and Catholics maintain that it is not the *only* one. Both sides cannot be right. And just as Protestants are passionate in defending *sola scriptura*, Catholics are equally passionate in defending the Church's Magisterium.

INFALLIBLE VS. INERRANT

Technically speaking, though Protestants use the word *infallible* to refer to Scripture, what they mean is *inerrant*. *Infallible* means "incapable of making a mistake" and applies most appropriately to people. *Inerrant* means "free from error" and applies to Scripture. Though some use the terms interchangeably, and though their meanings overlap to an extent, they are not synonymous. But for the sake of continuity, I will refer to Scripture as infallible, as Protestants do.

One positive thing about each position is that it proceeds from a desire to honor the scriptures and to safeguard the place they have in the life of the Church. Perhaps this is the common ground where Protestants and Catholics may yet reach further accord.

The Origin of *Sola Scriptura*

The doctrine that Scripture is the Christian's only infallible rule of faith was popularized and promoted by Martin Luther, who, the story goes, affixed his *Ninety-five Theses* to the church door at Wittenberg's Castle Church in 1517.[4] His *Theses* put forth a series of propositions for debate, focusing prominently on the doctrine of indulgences—see the *Catechism of the Catholic Church* (CCC), paragraph 1471—which he sought to challenge. Since indulgences are granted on the pope's authority, Luther's position led to his rejection of that authority, resulting in his corollary claim that only the Bible could be the ultimate guiding authority for Christians.

In 1577, the Formula of Concord, a Lutheran confessional statement, reaffirmed this standard:

> First[, then, we receive and embrace with our whole heart] the prophetic and apostolic scriptures of the Old and New Testaments as the pure, clear fountain of Israel, which is *the only true standard* by which all teachers and doctrines are to be judged.[5]

Along with *sola fide*, the belief that faith alone is necessary for salvation, *sola scriptura* became one of the two pillars of the Protestant Reformation.

Now, some of the abuses Luther reacted to were real, and he was justified in condemning them. Indeed, he was not the first to decry abuses in the Church—St. Francis of Assisi, St. Catherine of Siena, and Cardinal Francisco Ximénes de Cisneros (archbishop of Toledo), for example, who worked within the Church to improve it without overthrowing the Magisterium, might have a more reasonable claim to the title "reformer."* However, as the hostilities between Luther and the Church's hierarchy proceeded, the issues ultimately centered on the question of Church authority and—from Luther's perspective—whether the teachings of the Catholic Church and its magisterial authority are legitimate and binding rules of faith for Christians. As these confrontations intensified, and Luther became more deeply entrenched in his own beliefs, he accused the Magisterium of having corrupted Christian doctrine, and he rejected Sacred Tradition as an unwritten repository of divine revelation given to and mediated by the Church.

Was Luther's doctrine in fact the restoration of a biblical truth that had been obscured over time, or was it only his own false view of Christian authority? Luther was passionate about his beliefs, and he succeeded in spreading them, but these facts do not guarantee that they were valid. Jesus said that people will come in his name and "mislead many," no doubt by spreading doctrines that *appear* to be from him or by claiming to speak with his authority (Matt. 24:5, Mark 13:6, Luke 21:8). The apostle Paul notes that the believers at Corinth were submitting to "another Jesus" and "a different gospel." How? By *discarding apostolic authority and tradition* as the standard against which the true gospel is measured (2 Cor. 11:4). Mind you, Paul's second letter to the Corinthian church was written barely twenty-five years after Jesus' ascension! Even after so short a time, within living memory of Christ's earthly mission, believers could still go astray.

---

* There were quite a few other saints in the sixteenth century who contributed to the reform of the Catholic Church, including Teresa of Avila, Robert Bellarmine, Charles Borromeo, Francis de Sales, Ignatius of Loyola, Thomas More, and Philip Neri.

Today, as in the first century and the sixteenth, souls are at stake. Christians need certitude in doctrine as a safeguard against believing in bogus gospels.

The twenty-five reasons that follow will examine Luther's doctrine of *sola scriptura* on the basis of practical, logical, and historical considerations in an attempt to show that it is not a genuine truth from God. Rather, it is a false doctrine of men—and a particularly malevolent one at that—masquerading as biblical teaching.

As St. Francis de Sales once noted,

> St. Hilary says excellently, "Heresy is in the understanding, not in the Scripture, and the fault is in the meaning, not in the words," and St. Augustine: "Heresies arise simply from this, that good scriptures are ill understood, and what is ill understood in them is also rashly and presumptuously given forth." It is a true Michal's game; it is to cover a statue . . . with the clothes of David (1 Sam. 19:11–17). He who looks at it thinks he has seen David, but he is deceived; David is not there. Heresy covers up, in the bed of its brain, the statue of its own opinion in the clothes of Holy Scripture. . . . He who sees this doctrine thinks he has seen the holy word of God, but he is mistaken; it is not there. The words are there, but not the meaning.[6]

The doctrine of *sola scriptura* takes a top-down structure of authority that Christ put in place, presents it as corrupt and evil on the basis of Luther's claims and accusations, supplants it with the ultimate exaltation of the ego (since, at least for some Protestants, individual believers can determine for themselves what Scripture means), and uses Scripture itself to give it a veneer of credibility and create the illusion that the belief is divine in origin, as Francis (and Augustine) correctly noted.

With *sola scriptura* as his battle cry, Martin Luther fomented contempt for the Christ-given authority of the Church and then replaced it with . . . Luther—and the rest of the human race. This is a critical factor in understanding *sola scriptura* because, whatever Protestants may claim about "Scripture interpreting Scripture" or the Holy Spirit guiding believers who read it prayerfully, in real-life practice, the doctrine puts the self *above* Scripture, via the believer's alleged freedom to decide for himself. The human reader is made to stand in judgment of God's word.

PROTESTANT OBJECTION: Scripture is self-interpreting; therefore, the believer's private interpretation *is* what the Holy Spirit intended.

CATHOLIC RESPONSE: This assertion is problematic for several reasons. First, the Bible nowhere says it is self-interpreting (see Reason 10); rather, it explicitly states or shows that it is *not*. See for example 2 Chron. 17:7-9; Neh. 8:1-9; Matt. 13:18-23; Luke 24:27, 45; Acts 8:30-31, 18:11; 1 Tim. 4:13; and 2 Pet. 1:20, 3:16.

Second, it is hard to believe that all Christians will arrive at the same interpretation of any given Scripture passage. The thousands of Protestant denominations in existence and their disagreements on major doctrines—baptismal regeneration, the real presence of Christ in the Eucharist, sanctification, and eternal security, to name a few—show how this has played out. If Scripture interprets itself, why don't all Protestants agree on its meaning?

Third, you can easily test the veracity of this assertion by referring to passages such as Matthew 16:18, Mark 16:16, and John 6:53. The Protestant understanding of these passages is a novelty. Why doesn't it agree with how the Church has always understood them if Scripture is self-interpreting?

Fourth, Martin Luther disagreed with John Calvin and Ulrich Zwingli, two of his Protestant contemporaries, on major doctrines such as the Eucharist. Nor did Calvin and Zwingli agree with each other. How does one account for this discrepancy from the start of Protestantism?

Luther took the same approach elsewhere. In 1521, at an imperial assembly called the Diet of Worms, he said, "Unless I am convinced by Scripture and plain reason—I do not accept the authority of the popes and councils, for they have contradicted each other—my conscience is captive to the word of God. I cannot and I will not recant anything, for to go against conscience is neither right nor safe."[7]

In other words, since there is no other authority to interpret it, Scripture has to bow to Luther's intellect, will, and conscience—and to ours.

But it should be the other way around. The human heart—the seat and center of all the operations of life—is deceitful and corrupt (Jer. 17:9), and it has been hardened (Eph. 4:18). The human mind also has been darkened by sin (Rom. 1:21, Eph. 4:18) and needs renewal (Rom. 12:2). A conscience must be formed correctly (1 Tim. 1:5, 19; Heb. 9:14) and subject to the ultimate judgment of an agency set up by God. We therefore cannot trust these things on their own.

We must be guided by God through Scripture, *but never apart from the spiritual and theological authority he has paired with it.*

Jesus knew exactly what he was doing when he founded his Church: he was keeping our flawed intellects and consciences from leading us astray. His Church is guaranteed his divine guidance; our personal reading comprehension is not. But since Luther expressly rejected the authority of Christ's Church, he was left with only his ego to guide himself and others.

Jesus cares deeply about us, and he desires intimate fellowship with us. Just as he is the visible sign of the Father (John 14:8-9), his Church is the visible sign of him. This is, no doubt, why he explicitly gave the Church his authority. The doctrine of *sola scriptura*, however, diminishes that authority and distorts Jesus' arrangement.

Let us, therefore, examine the reasons why *sola scriptura* could not have originated with him.

PART I: THE REASONS

REASON 1

PROTESTANTS CANNOT AGREE ON A DEFINITION OF *SOLA SCRIPTURA*

Since the time of Martin Luther, multiple ways of defining *sola scriptura* have surfaced. This is problematic: not only do Protestants disagree with Catholics over *sola scriptura*, but they don't agree among themselves how to define the belief. If there is no uniform standard or definition used by all or even most Protestants, it can't be our sole rule of faith.

Protestant apologist James White notes how important it is to have accurate definitions:

> After engaging hundreds, possibly thousands of individuals over the sufficiency of Scripture, I have come to realize that 85 percent of the battle is fought over definitions. Few of the arguments against biblical sufficiency in matters of faith and morals are truly compelling *if* one is fully aware of the real issues.[6]

Catholic apologist Jimmy Akin confirms this lack-of-definition issue based on his own experience debating Protestants:

> One of the stickiest points in Catholic-Protestant debates is what is meant by the Protestant term *sola scriptura*, or "Scripture alone." Protestant apologists assert the doctrine but are often reluctant to offer a precise definition of it. Most will say that it does not mean certain things and will make a general stab at saying what it does mean, but I do not know of a Protestant apologist who has offered a complete and precise definition. . . .
>
> The problem is that there is no single Protestant position on *sola scriptura*. The term is used different ways, the details of which vary.[7]

Before becoming Catholic, Tim Staples was raised a Southern Baptist and became involved with various Assembly of God communities. He also notes that during his time as a Protestant, a clear and uniform definition of *sola scriptura* eluded him:

> Diving deeper into its meaning to defend my Protestant faith against Catholicism . . . I found that there was no uniform understanding of this teaching among Protestant pastors and no book I could read to get a better understanding of it.[8]

This lack of uniformity is not surprising. For some Protestants, Scripture is the *only* authority. For others, it is the only *infallible* authority. For others still, it is the only *final* authority, because they allow for other sources of information, such as the writings of the Church Fathers, to serve as historical and doctrinal references.

Some Protestants do try to offer coherent definitions of *sola scriptura*, of course. Not only do these definitions differ from one another, but each of them is flawed. Consider some examples.

The Bible Alone Is the Christian's Rule of Faith

"The doctrine of *sola scriptura*, simply stated, is that the scriptures and the scriptures alone are sufficient to function as the *regula fide*, the 'rule of faith' for the Church. All that one must believe to be a Christian is found in Scripture and in no other source. That which is not found in Scripture is not binding upon the Christian conscience."[9]

Problem #1: We know that the Church has known at least one other rule of faith—namely, apostolic teaching, which is definitely binding upon Christians. Moreover, Scripture doesn't ever say that apostolic teaching will cease to function as a rule of faith. We can look to Matthew 16:19, 18:18; Acts 15:22-29; 1 Corinthians 5:3-5; and 2 Timothy 2:1-2 for examples.

Problem #2: For *sola scriptura* to work, the canon of the Bible (the list of books that belong in it) must certainly be binding upon all Christians. But that list is not found anywhere in the Bible.

Problem #3: Certain distinctive characteristics of Christ's Church, such as its hierarchical structure and its sacramental system, *are* "found in Scripture" and hence are part of the rule of faith for Christians. How does an adherent to this definition of *sola scriptura* know when to apply this principle and when to ignore it?

PROBLEM #4: Saying that Scripture is "all that one must believe to be a Christian" doesn't specify if Scripture contains just those truths *necessary for salvation* or if it also contains *all the truths of Christian theology*. For example, the existence of angels is a theological truth we find in the Bible. But is it something we *must* believe in?

The famous nineteenth-century Baptist preacher Charles Spurgeon asserted that not all theological truths are of equal importance:

> We are not saved by knowing any one theological truth we may choose to think of, for there are some theological truths which are comparatively of inferior value. They are not vital or essential, and a man may know them, and yet may not be saved.[10]

If these truths are not vital, then the reverse may also be true: a person might not know them but still be saved. This invites Protestants to discard or downplay certain doctrines as being of "inferior value" based on their own judgment. Yet Jesus never gave his followers liberty to judge the value of a given biblical truth (Matt. 28:20). Jesus did not make optional any teachings in the Father's plan of redemption. To empower individual believers to do so would violate the integrity of God's revelation to humanity.

Problem #5: Since the essential parts of biblical revelation are not defined, what it means to be a Christian is not defined. If *sola scriptura* doesn't tell us how to know for sure that we're Christians, how can it be our sole rule of faith?

The Bible Alone Is the Primary and Absolute Source for All Doctrine

"By *sola Scriptura* Protestants mean that Scripture alone is the primary and absolute source for all doctrine and practice (faith and morals). *Sola scriptura* implies several things. First, the Bible is a direct *revelation* from God. As such, it has divine authority. . . . Second, the Bible is *sufficient*: it is all that is necessary for faith and practice. For Protestants 'the Bible alone' means 'the Bible only' is the final authority for our faith. Third, the scriptures not only have sufficiency, but they also possess *final authority*. They are the final court of appeal on all doctrinal and moral matters."[11]

Problem #1: The claim of sufficiency—that the Bible is "all that is necessary for faith and practice"—is disproved by Church history. We know that from the earliest centuries the Christian faithful relied—sometimes in a critical way—on what the Church affirmed and denied in its councils, especially when refuting the many heresies that threatened to pull Christians away from authentic apostolic teaching. It was the Church's Magisterium that provided doctrinal clarity, as evidenced by the numerous times it had to address heresies *that were based on Scripture*. In those instances, the implications of *sola scriptura* actually *created* disputes, and the Bible by itself could not be used to resolve them.

PROBLEM #2: The claim of an absolute source of authority is also refuted by the exercise of the Church's magisterial authority in its councils. The Church has always expected believers to accept what it promulgates as binding because it is the final court of appeal. Christians are not at liberty to go back to the Bible and judge a council's proceedings for themselves. That is not the mechanism Jesus set up to ensure doctrinal purity in his Church.

The Bible Alone Is Inerrant, Sufficient, and Final

"*Sola scriptura* declares that only Scripture is our inerrant, sufficient, and final authority for the church, because it is God-breathed and divinely inspired (2 Tim. 3:16)."[12]

PROBLEM #1: The Church has known more than one final authority in its history—namely, the apostles and their successors, who functioned as the final authority while the New Testament was being written and who continued exercising that authority beyond its completion.

PROBLEM #2: Divine inspiration would ensure inerrancy, but it does not follow that it would also ensure sufficiency and finality. The Old Testament gives us an example by way of prefiguring. The Torah was divinely inspired, but it did not function as the sufficient and final authority. The Jews also had their oral tradition and the seat of Moses—an authoritative office—working in conjunction with it. In a parallel way, the New Testament is also divinely inspired and thus inerrant, but Jesus intended for it to function with other authorities—namely Sacred Tradition and the Church's Magisterium.

Problem #3: All the teachings the apostles received from Jesus were divinely inspired. Some were passed on in written form and others in oral form (see 2 Thess. 2:15). Scripture contains only the written form and hence cannot be sufficient or final because it lacks the oral form, which became known as Sacred Tradition.

The Bible is the Supreme Authority, but Not the Only Authority

"*Sola scriptura* does not mean that the Bible is the only authority for believers. What then did the phrase *sola scriptura* mean at the time of the Reformation? . . . Firstly, *sola scriptura* meant Scripture was the supreme authority over the church. It did not mean Scripture was the only authority. Luther, Calvin, and the other Reformers used other authorities like reason and tradition. They developed arguments using logic (reason) and learned from the writings of past Christians (tradition) as they explored the Bible."[13]

Problem #1: This definition underscores how Protestants don't agree on one definition of *sola scriptura.*

Problem #2: If the assertions in this definition are true, then the modern definition of *sola scriptura*, at least for some groups, is not the same as the original definition. This change suggests two possibilities. First, the original definition may have been corrupted. But if *sola scriptura* is vulnerable to mutation, how can it serve as a consistent rule of faith across the centuries? Or, second, the change was intentional, which presupposes that making such a change is permissible and that the groups who do it have the requisite authority to initiate such a change. I'm not confident that other Protestant groups would agree.

The Bible Is the Only Infallible Rule, but Not All that Christians Need

"*Sola scriptura* means that Scripture is the only infallible rule of doctrine and practice for Christians today. . . . First, *sola scriptura* does not mean that the Bible is all Christians need to be saved or to live a faithful Christian life. 'Me and my Bible' is not a complete picture of the Christian life. . . . Second, *sola scriptura* does not mean a rejection of all tradition. The historic evangelical doctrine of *sola scriptura* is that taught by the Protestant Reformers of the sixteenth century such as Luther and Calvin, who held the traditions of Christianity, especially those of the early Church Fathers, generally in high esteem."[14]

Problem #1: This definition contradicts the idea of biblical sufficiency found in many other definitions of *sola scriptura*, once again pointing to the impracticality of a doctrine that can't be universally defined.

Problem #2: This author goes on to say that a Christian also "needs" the Holy Spirit, prayer, the Church, and corporate worship of God, along with the encouragement, instruction, exhortation, challenge, and rebuke of other believers, to live a "faithful Christian life." But if the Bible is meant to function *in concert with* these other things, it can't be the only rule for Christians.

Problem #3: If not all tradition is rejected, then some of it is legitimate. Not only is this the Catholic approach to tradition, but how does a Protestant know what content from the early Fathers to accept as legitimate and what to reject? Who makes that determination? Does this source speak authoritatively for all Protestants or just for some?

PROBLEM #4: If some tradition is legitimate and helps to "complete the picture" of Christian life, then based on the Protestant notion of *perspicuity* (sufficiently clear, able to be understood by anyone), valid tradition should be easy to determine. But the history of Protestantism seems to belie this claim, because not all Protestants agree on what constitutes valid tradition. Some, in fact, discard tradition altogether. Furthermore, how does a Christian know if tradition should function as a rule of faith or merely be held "in high esteem"?

PROBLEM #5: Very well: "Me and my Bible" is an incomplete picture. But how are we to know for sure what components are missing unless there is divine guidance or sanction to ensure that we have everything we need to be Christians? Jesus gave both these things to the Church he founded because the Church speaks with his authority . . . but this fact represents a grave problem for the doctrine of *sola scriptura*.

Based on the above definitions, the doctrine of *sola scriptura* attributes four defining characteristics to the Bible and its authority: *infallible*, *sole*, *final*, and *sufficient*. The two fundamental difficulties overall are that Protestants don't agree on which combination of them serves as the rule of faith, and Church history has shown conclusively that *sole*, *final*, and *sufficient* just aren't true. And the inherent problems with *sola scriptura* have only begun.

Questions to Ask:

1. Protestants have different definitions of *sola scriptura*. Which one is right? How do we know?

2. The New Testament shows the early Church's Magisterium functioning in Acts 15 (see Reason 2). When and why did that authority cease to function in the life of the Church? When was it supplanted by Scripture alone?

3. If the Protestant claim of supplantation is true, is there any clear indication of it in Scripture? What about in the writings of the early Church Fathers?

4. If *sola scriptura* is clearly taught in the Bible, why don't all Protestants agree on its definition?

5. Who decides which theological truths in Scripture are "essential" or "vital"? Who gave this person or group the authority to make such a determination?

6. If some tradition is legitimate, to what extent should it complete the "picture of Christian life," and how does a believer know this without ending up with an insufficient rule of faith?

REASON 2

THE FIRST CHRISTIANS DID NOT HAVE A BIBLE

The last book of the New Testament, Revelation, was not written until about the year A.D. 68.[15] That leaves a thirty-five-year gap between Jesus' ascension and the completion of the Bible as we know it. Can an incomplete Bible be the sole rule of faith?

Furthermore, if the doctrine of *sola scriptura* were true, then the Church would have existed for a time without its sole infallible rule of faith. During this time, there would have been controversies, doctrinal disputes, and other difficulties that could not be resolved. On the individual level, believers would have lacked the fullness of divine revelation. Both of these facts demonstrate a fatal flaw in the doctrine of *sola scriptura*, and we still have many more reasons to explore.

GOSPEL DATING

Some modern scholars date the Gospels and certain epistles, on average, about twenty to twenty-five years later than the dates given in this book. For instance, some assign a date of A.D. 90-100 for the Book of Revelation. In the informed opinion of this author, the earlier dates given by Jimmy Akin and other Bible scholars are more trustworthy. Moreover, if the later date is accurate, it would mean that the Church existed even longer without the New Testament as the final authority, thus weakening the Protestant position even further.

The first few decades of the Church's existence were turbulent. Persecutions had already begun, and more were imminent (Matt. 10:16–18, Luke 21:12, John 15:20–21, 2 Tim. 3:11–12, Rev. 2:10). Believers were being martyred (Acts 7:54-60, 12:1-2). The apostolic teaching was met with resistance (Acts 5:17-18, 27-28; 17:5-6, 13), and false teachings had already appeared (Acts 20:29-30, Gal. 1:6-9, 1 John 4:1). If the Bible was the Christian's only rule of faith at that time, and if the Bible was not fully written, by the earliest reckoning, until decades after Christ's ascension, how did early Christians deal with immediate threats to the new faith?

The New Testament answers this question. In Acts 15, we read about the Council of Jerusalem. The issue at hand was whether a believer had to be circumcised according to the Mosaic Law in order to be saved (v. 1). Luke tells us that "Paul and Barnabas had no small dissension and debate with them"—that is, those who were insisting on circumcision—but since the issue was still not settled, these two men were sent to Jerusalem to confer with the apostles and presbyters to put it to rest. "After there had been much debate," Peter stands up and delivers his ruling on the matter (vv. 7-11), after which "all the assembly kept silence."

This is a telling account, because conspicuously present is Peter's teaching authority, and conspicuously absent is an appeal to Scripture. In fact, those *in favor of* circumcision were the ones appealing to Scripture (vv. 1, 5), but Peter overruled them on the basis of his own power to teach on matters of faith. The Magisterium functioned exactly as Jesus had designed it to.

At this point in the life of the Church, *none* of the New Testament had been written yet. But there were still Christians who wanted authoritative Christian truth, who wanted to be saved. God didn't abandon them as casualties of a *sola scriptura* system that wouldn't be functional until long after they were dead. It doesn't seem reasonable, therefore, to think that even after Jesus revealed the fullness of the Father's plan, imparted his teachings to the apostles, and established his Church to be the means by which those teachings were brought to the world, there would be one group of people who lacked a rule of faith (no New Testament) and another group, much later, who had it once the New Testament was complete.

Protestant Objection: Christians necessarily had to wait until the completion of the New Testament. The apostles may have been the authority during that time, but once the New Testament was written and the Bible was complete, it replaced the apostles as the only rule of faith for believers.

Catholic Response: This claim is pure supposition and has no support in the New Testament. Aren't the important teachings of Scripture—like what transpires in the Council of Jerusalem, where the apostles demonstrate their binding authority—sufficiently clear, as Protestants claim? If *sola scriptura* is a central doctrine, why would it be based on inference at best and supposition at worst rather than being explicitly stated in Scripture?

Faced with the time gap between the Ascension and the completion of the New Testament, Protestants are left with three possibilities regarding temporary sources of Christian authority for that period: (1) *nothing*, (2) the *Old Testament*, or (3) the *apostles*.

Of course, having nothing as a rule of faith for Christians is untenable. It contradicts the passages where Jesus clearly gives his authority to the apostles, it leaves the Church vulnerable to the kinds of difficulties mentioned above, and it leaves no court of final appeal to settle the Church's internal and disciplinary matters.

The Old Testament by itself cannot serve as the rule of faith because it needs to be interpreted, as evidenced by the scenario just mentioned in Acts 15—or Luke 24, where Jesus has to explain to the two disciples walking to Emmaus "the things concerning himself" in "all the [Old Testament] scriptures" (v. 27) as well as to the disciples in Jerusalem (vv. 44-45). It functioned alongside the Jews' tradition and the seat of Moses, showing that in practice it was not a sole authority. And if it were sufficient for Christians, then the New Testament would not have needed to be written.

That leaves us with apostolic authority. Nowhere does the Bible indicate that it would be temporary—still less that it would give way to the authority of Scripture alone. On the contrary, we see that the apostles chose *successors*, who, in turn, possessed the same authority to "bind and loose" (render authoritative decisions) that they had. This is why Matthias was elected as a replacement for Judas Iscariot (Acts 1:15–26) and why Paul passed on his apostolic authority to Timothy and Titus (2 Tim. 1:6, Titus 1:5). If anything, pointing to the apostles to solve the authority gap supports the Catholic position: since Jesus intended his Church to exist until his return, he intended apostolic authority (the Church's Magisterium) to exist, as clearly evidenced by the selection of successors to their office.

Questions to Ask:

1. What was the final, infallible rule of faith for Christians living in the first century?

2. At the Council of Jerusalem, the converted Pharisees used the scriptures to assert that circumcision was a necessary prerequisite to being saved. Why weren't the scriptures used to settle the issue? What was the final authority that settled the issue being debated?

3. If the apostles were able to settle doctrinal disputes without the Bible, what does this say about the authority structure of Christ's Church? What does it suggest about *sola scriptura*?

4. If the scriptures are self-interpreting, as some Protestants believe, why would the apostles need to settle any doctrinal disputes in the first place?

5. If the scriptures are self-interpreting, why did the converted Pharisees in Acts 15 arrive at the wrong interpretation of the Mosaic Law?

6. Why couldn't Paul and Barnabas settle their debate by appealing to Scripture?

REASON 3

THE CHURCH PRODUCED THE BIBLE, NOT VICE VERSA

The doctrine of *sola scriptura* overlooks or at least downplays the fact that the Church not only came before the New Testament, but wrote its books and selected the canon of the entire Bible. For Catholics, both the Church and Scripture are infallibly authoritative, and hence the result is equal to the cause. The Spirit who inspired Scripture is the same Person who Christ promised would guide his Church to all truth.

Protestants who hold to *sola scriptura*, however, make the result greater than the cause. Somehow, an infallible work of the Spirit (Scripture) emerged from what Protestants say is a fallible institution (the Church). This seems to be a logical dilemma. Doesn't it make more sense to suggest that an infallible work was produced by an infallible institution, since both have the Holy Spirit's guidance? Why would he guide one important aspect of the Church and protect it from all error but allow the Church's teachings, some of which are based directly on Scripture, to potentially lapse into error or not have his guidance?

But Jesus gave primacy to the teaching authority of his Church and its proclamation of salvation in his name, not to printing and distributing a book—and most assuredly not to leaving individuals to interpret divine revelation for themselves. In practice, *sola scriptura* not only subordinates a cause (the Church) to an effect (Scripture), but then subordinates the effect to the decidedly fallible interpretation of those who read it.

The faithful are meant to *receive* the deposit of faith and submit to it, not judge it for themselves. The New Testament clearly attests that this is Christ's will for his Church:

> And Jesus came and said to them, "All authority in heaven and on earth has been given to me. Go therefore and make disciples of all nations, baptizing them in the name of the Father and of the Son and of the Holy Spirit, teaching them to observe all that I have commanded you; and lo, I am with you always, to the close of the age" (Matt. 28:18-20).

> And he said to them, "Go into all the world and preach the gospel to the whole creation. He who believes and is baptized will be saved; but he who does not believe will be condemned" (Mark 16:15-16).

> He who hears you hears me, and he who rejects you rejects me, and he who rejects me rejects him who sent me (Luke 10:16).

PROTESTANT OBJECTION: In the context of Luke 10, Jesus commissions seventy* disciples to announce his kingdom "to every town and place he intended to visit." The teaching commission, therefore, was for *all* disciples, not just the apostles, so there was nothing special about the apostles' (or the Church's) authority.

CATHOLIC RESPONSE: Although he wants all Christians to promote the gospel, Jesus gives his apostles special authority that he does not give to the faithful at large (e.g., the power to bind and loose, in Matt. 18:18). This authority was so vital to the Church that a new apostle, Matthias, had to be chosen to fill the void left by Judas (Acts 1:15-26). The earliest Christians understood this, and so "devoted themselves to the apostles' teaching and fellowship" (2:42).

And yet, interestingly, the seventy in Luke 10 *are* invested with Christ's authority, though in a lesser way than the apostles. They, too, demonstrate that Jesus wanted a specific body of teachings to be imparted to the world through instruction from human ministers. Whenever the New Testament talks about Jesus giving people a commission to evangelize the world, there is never even a hint that someday their authority will be superseded by a book that readers will interpret for themselves. From the start, evangelical proclamation and Christian instruction were governed and guided by legitimate ecclesial authority and approval.

---

* The footnote for Luke 10:1 in the New American Bible reads, "Important representatives of the Alexandrian and Caesarean text types read 'seventy,' while other important Alexandrian texts and Western readings have 'seventy-two.'"

Since the Catholic Church is the historical entity through which the Holy Spirit produced the New Testament, it is reasonable to say that it alone has the authority to interpret it. By producing the scriptures, the Church also needs to serve as their guardian and interpreter.

> The Church existed before the Bible; it made the Bible; it selected its books, and it preserved it. It handed it down; through it we know what is the word of God, and what is the word of man; and hence to try at this time of day, as many do, to overthrow the Church by means of this very Bible, and to put it above the Church, and to revile it for destroying it and corrupting it—what is this but to strike the mother that reared them; to curse the hand that fed them; to turn against their best friend and benefactor; and to repay with ingratitude and slander the very guide and protector who has led them to drain of the water out of the Savior's fountains?[16]

Protestant Objection: The scriptures are divinely inspired. They have the Holy Spirit as their author, and hence they stand above the Church.

Catholic Response: Such a claim effectively ignores or overlooks the Church's constitution. To say the scriptures are inspired means that the biblical writers were divinely guided so that what they wrote is God's word and is therefore infallible. The same things can be said about the Church. Jesus founded it with his explicit words in Matthew 16:18–19, and therefore it also has a divine origin. He gave his teachings—quite literally the word of God—to his Church, and they are also infallible. Jesus gave his authority to the apostles to teach in his name (Matt. 28:18-20), and he ensured that his teachings would remain inviolate by promising to always be with his Church (v. 20, John 14:18) and having the Holy Spirit guide it to all truth (John 15:26, 16:13).

The Church and the scriptures have the same essential constitution—divine origin, guidance, and content—so how can one of them possibly be subordinated to the other? The Church stands alongside the scriptures, not "below" them.

Questions to Ask:

1. If the scriptures are the only final, infallible authority in the life of Christians, how did the Church produce something greater than itself? If the Holy Spirit gave his infallible guidance for the writing of the New Testament books, why would he not also give his infallible guidance to the institution that produced them? Didn't Jesus send the Spirit to guide the apostles into all truth (John 16:13) and to safeguard the Church that Jesus founded?

2. Why should the Third Person of the Trinity, who inspired Scripture, be greater than the Second Person of the Trinity, who gave authority to the Church?

3. The Bible and the Church are both divine in origin. Since they both come from God, why should it be hard to believe that they both have authority?

4. The Holy Spirit guided the process of writing the New Testament. Has he also guided Christians over time to ensure that its contents are properly understood? If so, how?

5. By saying that the scriptures "stand above" the Church, how do we avoid the inevitable result of this claim—namely, diminishing the Church's authority to speak in Jesus' name? Are Christians at liberty to challenge, question, or downplay the authority Jesus gave to his Church?

REASON 4

THE EARLY CHURCH LINKED SCRIPTURAL AND MAGISTERIAL AUTHORITY

The early Church Fathers—bishops and theologians of the first few centuries A.D.—are important witnesses to the beliefs and practices of Christians in the time immediately following the apostles. In their writings, you will see explicit references to the primacy and authority of Rome, apostolic succession, and bishops as stewards of the deposit of faith. The early Church did not operate according to *sola scriptura*. Rather, it had a hierarchy that the early followers of Christ acknowledged, to which they subjected themselves in matters of faith.

Consider a few examples of what the early Fathers said about the Magisterium and its role in the life of Christians:

> If . . . any shall disobey the words spoken by him through us, let them know that they will involve themselves in transgression and serious danger (Pope Clement, Letter to the Corinthians, 59).

> See that you all follow the bishop, even as Jesus Christ does the Father, and the presbytery as you would the apostles; and reverence the deacons, as being the institution of God. Let no man do anything connected with the Church without the bishop (Ignatius of Antioch, Letter to the Smyrnaeans, 8).

> As therefore the Lord did nothing without the Father, being united to him, neither by himself nor by the apostles, so neither do anything without the bishop and presbyters (Ignatius of Antioch, Letter to the Magnesians, 7).

> We do put to confusion all those who, in whatever manner, whether by an evil self-pleasing, by vainglory, or by blindness and perverse opinion, assemble in unauthorized meetings; [we do this, I say,] by indicating that tradition derived from the apostles, of the very great, the very ancient, and universally known Church founded and organized at Rome by the two most glorious apostles, Peter and Paul; as also [by pointing out] the faith preached to men, which comes down to our time by means of the successions of the bishops. For it is a matter of necessity that every Church should agree with this Church, on account of its preeminent authority (Irenaeus, *Against Heresies*, 3:3:2).

These words were written within the first 150 years or so after Jesus' resurrection and ascension. If *sola scriptura* were the Christians' rule of faith, it would be exceedingly odd that such binding authority is affirmed as belonging to the Magisterium as well—and so early on in the Church's existence. It is also noteworthy that no one challenged such words as being inconsistent with the authority structure Jesus put in place for his Church.

Rather than individual believers deriving doctrine from personal interpretation of an infallible book, which is what we would expect to find if *sola scriptura* were true, the Fathers have consistently witnessed to a threefold authority structure: Scripture, Tradition, and the Magisterium, with each component existing alongside of and functioning in concert with the other two.

The Second Vatican Council, in its Dogmatic Constitution on Divine Revelation, affirmed this arrangement:

> It is clear, therefore, that Sacred Tradition, Sacred Scripture, and the teaching authority of the Church, in accord with God's most wise design, are so linked and joined together that one cannot stand without the others, and that all together and each in its own way under the action of the one Holy Spirit contribute effectively to the salvation of souls (*Dei Verbum* 10).

This was in keeping with Old Testament precedent. In the Jewish faith community, there was also a threefold authority structure: the Mosaic Law, their oral tradition, and the teaching authority of Moses and his successors (the "seat of Moses"). It makes perfect sense that the Old Testament authority would prefigure that of the New, since both come from God.

The Protestant authority model, by contrast, consists of only one component.

A modern comparison could be made with civil authority. In America, we have a government that consists of three branches: executive, judicial, and legislative. If *solo lex* ("only law") were true, then it would follow that society needs only written laws, without governors to enact them or courts to interpret them. Citizens could just consult a library of legal books and figure out for themselves how to understand and apply our laws.

But such an arrangement is absurd. No one could possibly expect civil society to function this way. There would be chaos. So why do Protestants think that Christianity can function this way?

Have we not seen chaos resulting since the sixteenth century? The splintering of Christianity in Europe immediately following the Reformation shows the social and spiritual disorder that *sola scriptura* fostered. Martin Luther himself complained that, in places where Church authority had been rejected,

> it is our daily experience that . . . the people entertain greater and bitterer hatred and envy and are worse with their avarice and money-grabbing than before under the papacy. . . . All boast that they are Christians, all are proud of their Christian liberty. Yet meantime they give way to concupiscence and turn to avarice, lust, pride, envy, etc. Nobody does his duty faithfully, nobody serves his neighbor in charity; sometimes this makes me so impatient, that I often wish those hogs that trample the pearls under foot, were still under the tyranny of the pope. . . .
>
> As everybody sees, the people are now more miserly, more merciless, more impure, more impudent, than before under the papacy. All vices, sins and infamies have become so common that they are no longer reputed as such. The people feel they are free

> from the bonds and fetters of the pope, but now they want to get rid also of the Evangelium and of all the laws of God.[17]

Here Luther seems sincere in his disappointment, but it is he who gave people license to interpret Scripture for themselves. How could he be surprised that people took his teachings to heart and followed his lead? Wasn't that exactly what he wanted them to do?

Questions to Ask:

1. Why does the Protestant model of the Church reject Christian authority components that the early Church Fathers accepted?

2. If you believe that the Old Testament is fulfilled in Christianity, doesn't it make sense that its authority structure would prefigure and parallel that of the Church—especially since God the Father always announces or prefigures what he is going to do?

3. If the threefold authority structure described by the early Church Fathers is invalid, as Protestants claim, that means the Holy Spirit allowed Christ's Church to abandon its sole rule of faith shortly after Jesus ascended to heaven. How likely is it that this happened?

4. Martin Luther himself noted that the result of his teachings was a dramatic increase in lawlessness and immorality. Does this suggest that he was guided by the Holy Spirit?

5. If *sola scriptura* is the Christian's sole rule of faith, how could the Church Fathers have written about the binding authority of the Magisterium, and why did no one formally challenge their doing so?

REASON 5

THE CANON OF THE BIBLE WAS NOT SETTLED UNTIL THE FOURTH CENTURY

An insurmountable problem for the doctrine of *sola scriptura* centers on one historical fact: that the canon of the Bible—the authoritative list of books that are inspired Scripture—was not fixed until the end of the fourth century.

Until that time, theologians had debated which writings were considered inspired and apostolic in origin. Some proposed lists had books that were later left out of the canon, whereas other lists omitted books that were later defined as canonical. There were early Christian writings thought by some to be inspired and apostolic that were even read in the liturgy—but were later omitted from the New Testament canon, including the *Didache*, the Epistle of Barnabas, and the Shepherd of Hermas.[18]

It was not until the Synod of Rome (382) and the Councils of Hippo (393) and Carthage (397 and 419) that a definitive canonical list was made, and each of these councils acknowledged the same list of books.* In addition, Pope Innocent I, writing in response to a request from Bishop Exsuperius of Toulouse in 405, put forth a canonical list that consisted of the same books as put forth by these four councils. From this point on, there is no variation in the canon of the Bible.

Protestant Objection: These councils are not ecumenical councils; therefore, they have no binding force on Christians.

Catholic Response: First, this objection implicitly admits that the proceedings of an ecumenical council are indeed binding on Christians—that is, that they serve as a *rule of faith*. Second, although it is true that these were not ecumenical councils, they give clear witness to the fact that the canon was not settled until more than 350 years after Christ.

The significant problem for Protestants here is that *sola scriptura* could not have functioned for the first 350-plus years of the Church's existence, because the doctrine is inextricably linked to the biblical canon. You can't claim "only Scripture" as the

---

* "This list is the same as the one given in the Church's final, definitive, explicit, infallible declaration as to which books are to be included in the Bible, which was made by the Council of Trent, Session IV, in 1546. Earlier lists of canonical books were the list in the 'Decretal of Gelasius,' which was issued by authority of Pope Damasus in 382, and the canon of Pope St. Innocent I, which was sent to a Frankish bishop in 405. Neither document was intended to be an infallible statement binding the whole Church, but both documents include the same seventy-three books as the list of the Council of Trent in the mid-sixteenth century" (*The Catholic Encyclopedia* [New York: The Encyclopedia Press, 1913], Vol. 3, 272).

sole rule of faith for Christians if you cannot also establish the contents of Scripture.

But a Protestant's *significant* problem turns into an *enormous* problem when you consider that the Protestants of the sixteenth century changed the canon that had been in place by that time *for over 1,100 years*.

ECUMENICAL COUNCILS

An ecumenical council is one in which the entire Church is represented (all bishops are called to participate) for the purpose of discussing and regulating Church doctrine and practice or discipline. Its decrees, once they are ratified by the pope or his legate, are considered infallible, and they are binding upon all Christians. To date, there have been twenty-one of them.

This is a fatal blow to *sola scriptura*: by changing the canon, Luther, Calvin, and others effectively claimed—from their perspective—that it had been wrong all that time. The inescapable, logical implication of this change is that *sola scriptura* had failed to function not only for the first 350-plus years of the Church's existence, but also for a mind-blowing 1,500-plus years! In other words, in Luther's and Calvin's day, *sola scriptura* had failed the Church *for its entire existence*, because the correct contents of the canon were not known until Luther and the other Protestants came along and asserted their version. In his absolute best-case scenario, Luther could claim only that *sola scriptura* began to function in the sixteenth century, once he had "set things right" with regard to the biblical canon.

To get around this obstacle, some Protestants will go to great lengths to distort the canon issue. James White, for instance, says,

> If the canon is nothing more than the table of contents, then it is a purely human thing, known by men and hence subject to all the endless debates and arguments history presents as having already taken place in almost every generation.[19]

This line of reasoning creates an artificial distinction between what White calls canon^1, "the *divine* knowledge and understanding of the canon," and canon^2, "the *human* knowledge and understanding of the canon (which has been the primary focus of debate down through the centuries)."

> Note something else as well: *Canon^1 exists whether or not canon^2 exists.* Canon^1 is necessary, while canon^2 is based solely upon God's desire to make known the extent of his act of revelation. Theoretically, God could keep canon^1 to himself, leaving the world in utter darkness concerning what is and is not inspired. And even as God leads his people to gain knowledge of canon^2, *there can be times when the certain knowledge of canon^2 lags behind the actual content of canon^1.* The knowledge of canon^2 is dependent upon God's purposes at any given point in time, and if his intentions include using a human process in the creation of canon^2, that process may not result in a clear and widely known canon listing for some time *after* the giving of that revelation.

There are multiple problems here:

- The artificial dichotomy between canon^1 and canon^2 admits that the human limits of knowledge of canon^2 could distort or diminish canon^1, effectively nullifying the reason why God would disclose the contents of the canon in the first place.
- The claim that debates about the canon have "taken place in almost every generation" is exaggerated. Sure, such debates took place for the first 350-plus years of the Church's existence, but as we have seen, those debates were settled—five times over the span of roughly forty years at the end of the fourth century.
- The canon *is* the biblical table of contents. It does not need to be morphed into anything else. Creating a second layer of meaning to it only adds to the confusion, because it introduces another topic over which "endless debates" can occur.
- We cannot know God's purposes except through his revelation, and we must therefore know which books actually contain his revelation.
- We see that "knowledge of canon^2 is dependent upon God's purposes at any given point in time," but God's purposes never change (Mal. 3:6, Heb. 13:8). Hence, our knowledge of canon^2 would never need to change, and neither would God need to withhold or dole out portions of canon^1 at any time. The fullness of divine revelation was embodied in Christ and his teachings, and the Holy Spirit ensured that its *written* component was completed in the Apostolic Age by inspiring the

books of the New Testament. The process of *identifying* the canon took long enough, but it essentially involved sifting through the same list of books, with some of them being identified as canonical later than others. If God kept giving the Church portions of the canon[1] at a time, how would the Church have even known when the canon was finally closed?

- The Church experienced a significant period of time in which "a clear and widely known canon listing" did not exist—namely, from Jesus' ascension to the turn of the fourth century. From the Protestant point of view, this would mean that Jesus left his Church without an infallible authority for more than 350 years.

Questions to Ask:

1. How can *sola scriptura* exist without a definitive—and infallible—identification of the biblical canon?

2. Was the biblical canon not properly identified until the sixteenth century? If so, why did the Holy Spirit wait so long to reveal it to the Church, and how could *sola scriptura* function without it in the meantime?

3. Where are the "endless debates" in the 1,100-plus years that passed between the settling of the canon at the end of the fourth century and the change of it by Protestants in the sixteenth century?

4. If the Church didn't have the authority to identify a canon of seventy-three books in the fourth and fifth centuries, why did the Protestant Reformers have the authority to identify a canon of sixty-six books in the sixteenth century?

5. Some Protestants maintain that the Bible is "a fallible collection of infallible books." Does this mean that the biblical canon hasn't actually been settled or closed? Is it possible that we will add or subtract from the canon in the future? Why or why not?

6. If *sola scriptura* were true and if the canon were in fact fallible, wouldn't Christians always be uncertain about whether they have the right books in their Bibles, right down to Jesus' Second Coming? Why would he leave his

Church in such uncertainty for all time, especially when the most important doctrine (from the Protestant perspective) is at stake?

7. If there are times when "certain knowledge of canon^{2} lags behind the actual content of canon^{1}," it means that canon^{2} at any time can be deficient, leaving the Church with a partial rule of faith and—worse still—no way to know what is missing. Is this situation tenable?

8. Did anything else supplement the Christian's rule of faith in those periods when canon^{1} and canon^{2} didn't coincide? If not, then the Church was still left with a partial rule of faith. Wouldn't that undermine *sola scriptura*?

REASON 6

AN EXTRABIBLICAL AUTHORITY IDENTIFIED THE CANON OF THE BIBLE

The Bible did not come with an inspired table of contents, so the doctrine of *sola scriptura* creates another dilemma for Protestants: how to know which books belong in the Bible—especially the New Testament. We cannot know (or agree on) this unless there is an outside source to tell us. Moreover, this source must be authoritative and infallible, since *sola scriptura* can't work if the Bible has errant books in it. But if such an infallible authority exists, then that fact alone repudiates the doctrine of *sola scriptura*.

More problematic still for Protestants, it is a historical fact that the Catholic Church identified the canon of the Bible. The councils we discussed above were all Catholic councils. When the Catholic Church gave its definitive and infallible definition of the biblical canon at the Council of Trent in 1546—acting in response to the Reformers' insistence on a different canon—it named the same seventy-three books that it had identified from the fourth century on, because the Holy Spirit has been consistent in his guidance of Christ's Church.

Protestant Objection: The Church did not create the canon; it *received* it. God alone is the author of the canon, and he did not have to depend on the Church's authority to validate it.

Catholic Response: Catholics agree that God alone is the author of the canon. We would even agree that the Church did not validate the canon in the sense that God needed the Church's approval of it, but we absolutely affirm that God used the Church's authority to correctly *identify* the canon. We further hold that only a visible institution founded by Jesus (Matt. 16:18), with the Holy Spirit working within it to preserve it from error (John 16:13), could ensure that the right books, and only the right books, would be identified as Scripture.

Faced with the problem of claiming that the Bible is the sole rule of faith while rejecting the authority that established the canon of the Bible, some Protestants resort to the claim that the Bible is "a fallible collection of infallible books." The implication is that the Protestant canon *could* be wrong—containing non-inspired books or omitting books that are inspired—but we have faith that it's not.

"A FALLIBLE COLLECTION"

The saying "a fallible collection of infallible books" is attributed to R.C. Sproul, a Presbyterian pastor and theologian, who founded Ligonier Ministries. James Swan, on his "Beggars All" website, suggests that the quote may have actually come from Sproul's teacher, John Gerstner. For our purposes, it doesn't really matter with whom the quote originated. The fact is that Protestants accept the idea.

But this position seems fatal for *sola scriptura*. If the Protestant Bible omits inspired books, then the sole rule of faith is incomplete, potentially leaving out teachings critical for salvation. If the Protestant Bible contains non-inspired works, then it is the basis for teaching both truth and error, meaning that the Protestant Bible fails at the task for which the doctrine of *sola scriptura* says it was designed.

Protestant Objection: The fact that our canon *might* be wrong doesn't have to mean that it *is* wrong. We believe that the Bible actually does contain the right books.

Catholic Response: Your faith is admirable, but you cannot have it both ways. The doctrine of *sola scriptura* doesn't let you treat the Bible as potentially wrong and functionally right simultaneously. Uncertainty and assurance are mutually exclusive realities. The fact is that you maintain such an untenable position because the Protestant belief system forces you to go to great lengths to avoid acknowledging the Catholic Church's authority and role in identifying the canon.

In effect, you're saying that the Church didn't have the authority to identify the canon because according to *sola scriptura*, it can't have that authority. But we must trust that the canon is somehow correct, because *sola scriptura* needs a correct canon to work. The doctrine forces you into a logical corner.

For a moment, let's go back to the Protestant idea of a "fallible collection of infallible books." James Swan, who hosts a comprehensive Protestant apologetics website called "Beggars All," says,

> For me to admit that the Bible is an "infallible collection" is really only a way of being cornered into admitting the Roman Catholic paradigm of an infallible extrabiblical authority. Does that therefore mean that I believe the Bible contains a book it shouldn't? No.[20]

Swan's premises are correct, but he resists the force of his own conclusion. He rejects any possibility of distortion in the process of the Church receiving the canon—as *sola scriptura* requires—suggesting divine guidance. But he can't admit to the divine guidance of the Church.

Protestants usually skirt this issue because they sense the implications that Swan has articulated: he accepts the infallible identification of the canon but rejects the agency by which it was made known—the Catholic Church.

He can't have it both ways. He doesn't believe that the Bible contains a book that it shouldn't (though he doesn't say if it lacks a book it should contain), but for this to be true, the canon must have been infallibly defined. Otherwise, he is just affirming his personal opinion, and this can't be the basis for the rule of faith for all Christians.

Swan goes on to say,

> I recognize the Christian church received the canon. It does not, though, create the canon, or stand above the canon. In other words, I see no reason to grant the Church infallibility in order for the Church to receive the canon. The Church was used by God to provide a widespread knowledge of the canon. The Holy Spirit had worked among the early Christian church in providing them with the books of the New Testament. This same process can be seen with the Old Testament and Old Testament believers. The Old Testament believer fifty years before Christ was born had a canon of Scripture, this despite the ruling from an infallible authority.

The relevant concerns here are these:

- The idea that the Church created the canon is a red herring. The Catholic Church does not claim to have done this. But since the scriptures are intended by God to be an integral component of the Church, *some* agency had to properly identify them. It makes perfect sense for God to have used the agency that his Son founded and that speaks with his Son's authority, especially considering that all of the New Testament books were written by members of that agency.
- If the Church did not infallibly identify the canon, then Christians have no way of knowing if the Bible they have can function as the rule of faith, because it may be missing books or it may have books in it that

shouldn't be there. In order for *sola scriptura* to function, the Church *must* have an infallibly defined canon.

- Swan acknowledges that the Church was a key factor in spreading knowledge of the canon, yet historically speaking, the canon it consistently affirmed was not the one that Luther redefined in his day. But we can't have it both ways: we cannot say the Church was instrumental in disseminating the canon and at the same time had a deficient canon.
- Swan and all Protestants affirm the same twenty-seven books of the New Testament that were identified by the Catholic Church and, in so doing, tacitly acknowledge its authority and the exercise of it. Even though Swan claims that the Church doesn't need infallibility to "receive the canon," he apparently doesn't for a moment question its ruling here on the canon issue. It would be an impossible task for anyone to defend the claim either that the New Testament is missing books or that more may yet be identified.

"I see no reason to grant the Church infallibility in order for the Church to receive the canon."

Then the Church has no guarantee that what it has "received" is the full list of correct books, and believers are left in a bind. Logically speaking, you cannot build an infallible proposition (we do, in fact, have the correct list of biblical books) upon a fallible basis (the Church is not infallible and therefore may have the wrong list).

"The Church was used by God to provide widespread knowledge of the canon."

This is a tacit admission that the Church is not only a visible entity established by Christ—the Catholic definition of "Church"—but also inextricably linked to the scriptures. But Swan rejects the authority of this Church, and even though that "widespread knowledge" was disseminated for 1,100-plus years and consisted of seventy-three books in the Bible, he violates his own claim by possessing and defending a deficient Bible that contains only sixty-six books.

"The Holy Spirit had worked among the early Christian Church in providing them with the books of the New Testament."

Exactly. And it was this same Holy Spirit that Jesus promised to his Church as the guarantor of truth and of all that he taught his apostles. It was also the leaders or important figures of the Catholic Church who authored these books.

Furthermore, although Swan accepts the Catholic Church's canon of New Testament books—his Bible has the same number of books as a Catholic Bible—he does so with an explicit rejection of its authority to speak in Christ's name. That doesn't make much sense. He accepts its authority in one important regard—in fact, central to Protestants—yet rejects it in others.

There is no other Church-issued list or change in the list of canonical books in any council, ecumenical or otherwise, from the early fourth century forward. If you include the ecumenical councils of Second Nicaea (787) and Florence (1431-1445), then you have seven instances when the same canon was identified before the Council of Trent came along and formally reaffirmed the canon in the wake of the Protestants' attempts to change it. So, long before Martin Luther changed the canon on his own authority—violating *sola scriptura* in the process—the Catholic Church had a clear and consistent history of affirming that the Bible contains seventy-three books, not sixty-six.

Questions to Ask:

1. If the Catholic Church can render an authoritative and infallible decision on which books belong in the Bible, then why reject its authority on other matters of faith?

2. Was the Church wrong about the canon for more than 1,100 years, until Luther fixed it? If so, how could Jesus have let Christians follow a sole rule of faith with errors—and for so long?

3. Why is it reasonable to believe that the Holy Spirit guided the Church vis-à-vis the New Testament and the biblical canon, but not that the Holy Spirit guides the Church in interpreting Scripture and teaching true doctrine?

4. If we know that the canon doesn't have non-inspired books in it, doesn't that mean that it was infallibly chosen? How did that happen?

5. If we don't know the canon's integrity, then how can a questionable standard be used as the sole rule of faith for Christians? Why would the Holy Spirit have allowed this?

6. Could more books of the New Testament be identified? If so, then how could *sola scriptura* have functioned up to now without them? If not, then hasn't the canon been infallibly defined?

REASON 7

THE MAIN CREEDS OF THE EARLY CHURCH DO NOT REFLECT *SOLA SCRIPTURA*

The creeds of the early Church are summaries of the principal articles of the Christian faith. The main creeds of the Catholic Church are the Apostles' Creed, the Athanasian Creed, and the Nicene Creed. Although not all Christians expressly adhere to these creeds, a large number do.

Immediately noticeable about these creeds is their failure to mention the doctrine of *sola scriptura*—or even a Bible. This is a glaring omission for Protestants. If the scriptures are Christians' only infallible authority, it seems inconceivable that they would be excluded from these early formulations of faith.

From the Catholic point of view, this omission makes sense, because we believe that Jesus left a living authority to teach, sanctify, and govern in his name until he returns. He did not instruct the apostles to write gospels or letters, or to make copies of the scriptures to hand out to Christians as personal rules of faith.

These facts are quite telling. To illustrate their implications, consider something that James White said in attempting to defend *sola scriptura*:

> Paul gives Timothy [in 2 Tim. 3] no indication that God will someday banish false teachers from disturbing the saints, at least not until that final day when the bride will be presented to her husband "having no spot or wrinkle" (Eph. 5:27). So what is Timothy to do, now that Paul will no longer be there to give him guidance?
>
> If ever there was a point where the apostle would refer to some kind of extrabiblical source of sufficiency, it would be here. If Paul believed we should look to a papacy, or to some Spirit-led prophet, or to some group of leaders, or to some new source of revelation, this would be the place to delineate this all-important source of aid for his beloved Timothy.[21]

White goes on to say that what Paul did instead was direct Timothy to the scriptures, and hence the doctrine of *sola scriptura* is affirmed. There are two considerations, however, that White overlooks.

1) In the context of 2 Timothy 3, when Paul mentions "the scriptures," he is referring to the books of the *Old* Testament, which was the only recognized Bible that existed at the time. Presumably, even White would agree that the Old Testament is insufficient to function as the *regula fide* in the life of Christians.

Protestant Objection: Paul is discussing the nature of Scripture—that is, a written work inspired ("God-breathed" is the meaning of the word in Greek) by the Holy Spirit. He is not discussing the canon.

Catholic Response: You cannot know what Scripture is—that is, you cannot know what is inspired—until you have the correct list of books that it comprises.

2) Paul had also imparted his *apostolic teaching and authority* to Timothy:

> Now you have observed my teaching, my conduct, my aim in life, my faith, my patience, my love, my steadfastness. . . . As for you, continue in what you have learned and have firmly believed, knowing from whom you learned it. (2 Tim. 3:10, 14).

The scriptures coupled with apostolic teaching authority is the Catholic position. Even in a passage cited to support *sola scriptura*, we see Paul appealing not only to Scripture, but also to apostolic teaching authority—three times in four verses!

We might borrow some of White's language in observing that if ever there was a time in the life of the Church when it would refer to the scriptures as the only infallible rule of faith for Christians, it would surely be in its creeds, since they articulate the principal teachings of Christianity in summarized form. If the early Christians had received the doctrine of *sola scriptura* from the apostles and Jesus, surely the creeds would have been the obvious place to delineate this all-important teaching for the Church's members.

Perhaps these early creeds support *sola scriptura* indirectly? Let's look at the relevant portions of each one.

Apostles' Creed (A.D. 120-150)

"I believe in the Holy Spirit, the holy catholic Church, the communion of saints."

THE APOSTLES' CREED

Scholars debate when this creed was actually written. Tradition maintains that each one of the twelve apostles wrote one statement of belief. A more realistic view is that the creed accurately summarizes apostolic teaching. The creed "is based on the baptismal profession of the early Roman Church" (see "Which Creed Came First, Apostles' or Nicene?", Catholic Answers) and hence is probably older than the Nicene Creed. A number of scholars hold that in its earliest form, it was developed in the second century.

Scripture isn't mentioned in this creed—but the Church is. It is clear that the leaders of the early Church wanted to emphasize in the life of believers the importance of the organization that Jesus founded, and it is also clear that the doctrine of *sola scriptura* was not in the minds of those leaders. Its absence in this creed would be a significant omission—in fact, inconceivable—if *sola scriptura* were the rule of faith that Protestants claim it to be.

Some Protestants will hedge here and attempt to define "catholic Church" as a general reference to the invisible community of all believers rather than to the Catholic Church we have today. And yet, historically speaking, at the time these creeds were written, there was only one "catholic Church," and it was a particular and visible entity with a hierarchical structure that had its headship in Rome. This Church can be traced forward in unbroken continuity to today's Catholic Church.

St. Ignatius of Antioch, in his Epistle to the Smyrnaeans, dated circa A.D. 107, said the following:

> Wherever the bishop shall appear, there let the multitude [of the people] also be; even as, wherever Jesus Christ is, there is the Catholic Church (8).

Catholics readily acknowledge the meaning of *catholic*—that is, "universal." We also assert that when Ignatius was referring to the "Church" that was "universal" in its scope, he was clearly referring to the *only* Church existing at that time. His description of Christ's Church became a proper name for it.

Yes, *catholic* means "universal," and that is what the Church Jesus founded was already becoming as Catholics went out into the world with the gospel. Protestants, in their efforts to justify their split from Christ's Church, attempt to change the meaning of "Catholic Church" from a proper noun identifying a historical, visible entity to a mere abstract concept.

Nicene Creed (325 and 381)

"I believe in one, holy, catholic, and apostolic Church."[22]

THE NICENE CREED

The earlier version of the Nicene Creed was shorter. The later version, which is familiar to and used by most Christians, was further developed at the Council of Constantinople in 381.

This is an explicit proclamation of the four *marks* (inherent, identifying characteristics) of the Church: *oneness* or unity, *holiness*, *catholicity*, and *apostolicity*. "Biblicality" is not mentioned. The Christians who composed this creed didn't think to subject the Church to a scriptural test.

The scriptures *are* mentioned in this creed, but only in connection with Jesus' resurrection:

> For our sake he was crucified under Pontius Pilate, he suffered death and was buried, and rose again on the third day in accordance with the scriptures.

The events that led to the formulation of the Nicene Creed are also telling. In brief, a Libyan priest named Arius denied that God the Son is equal (*consubstantial*) with God the Father and asserted instead that he is a created being. The spread of Arius's teachings caused such theological and civil unrest that the Council of Nicaea was convened, in major part, to address them. At the council, Arius was soundly condemned as a heretic, "the confession of faith which he presented was torn in pieces,"[23] his writings were burned, and he was exiled to Illyria.

This is noteworthy for us because *Arius was basing his false teachings on Scripture.*[24] The Magisterium of the Church, present in the council fathers under the authority of the pope, was needed as the final rule to settle a controversy caused by private interpretation of Scripture!

Athanasian Creed (c. 361, and possibly late fifth century)

"Whosoever will be saved, before all things it is necessary that he hold the catholic faith . . . and the catholic faith is this . . . which except a man believe faithfully he cannot be saved."[25]

THE ATHANASIAN CREED

Though ascribed to St. Athanasius, the bishop of Alexandria, modern scholarship holds that he was probably not its author, though it certainly has Athanasian influences. As with the Apostles' Creed, there is not a scholarly consensus on its date of composition. For more information, see the *Catholic Encyclopedia* article at https://www.newadvent.org/cathen/02033b.htm.

Though this creed deals chiefly with the doctrines of the Trinity and the Incarnation, it has oblique references to the teaching authority of Christ's Church, which is the agency that defines, teaches, and safeguards what is contained in "the catholic faith." Once again, Scripture is not mentioned.

We can add the Chalcedonian Creed (451) for good measure. Though this creed focuses on the two natures of Christ, it begins and ends with a reference to "the holy Fathers" who constitute the Magisterium of the Catholic Church.

> We, then, following the holy Fathers, all with one consent, teach men to confess one and the same Son, our Lord Jesus Christ . . . as the prophets from the beginning [have declared] concerning him, and the Lord Jesus Christ himself has taught us, and the creed of the holy Fathers has handed down to us.[26]

This is a most telling reference, because the faith being handed down depends on what "the holy Fathers" teach, not what the scriptures mean according to our own reading. Of course, what the "holy Fathers" teach is informed by God's revelation in inspired Scripture.

The Bible is vital to the Church. But distortion occurs when Protestants assert that the scriptures are meant to function *alone*, without the Church's teaching authority wielding them.

This excerpt also emphasizes the Catholic doctrine of Tradition: what has been "handed down" by our apostolic fathers in the Faith, who, in turn, handed it down to others.

Questions to Ask:

1. If the doctrine of *sola scriptura* is true and is as important as Protestants allege, why do the main creeds of the early Church fail to mention it? Why do they not talk about the authority of the Bible at all?

2. Does the consistent mention of "the Church" or "the holy Fathers" in these creeds support the Protestant position or the Catholic position?

3. The Nicene Creed was formulated in direct response to the Arian heresy. If biblical meaning is sufficiently clear on its own, as some versions of *sola scriptura* claim, how did Arius misinterpret it on such a critical doctrine as the divinity of Christ? How did so many people, including patriarchs and emperors, become Arians?

4. What was used to authoritatively refute Arius's position: Scripture alone or an interpretation of Scripture, as officially set forth by the Catholic Church at a council?

5. Was the teaching of the Council of Nicaea on Christ's divinity binding on Christians, or are Christians today free to dismiss it? If it's the latter, then why?

REASON 8

SOLA SCRIPTURA DID NOT EXIST UNTIL THE FOURTEENTH CENTURY

It stands out that one of the core doctrines of Protestantism did not exist prior to the fourteenth century (with John Wycliffe), and it did not become prevalent until the sixteenth century (with Martin Luther). To put it bluntly, *sola scriptura* simply did not exist before about 1,200 years after the last of the apostles had died.

WYCLIFFE AND HUS

John Wycliffe (1330-1384) was an English priest, theologian, and seminary professor. Jan Hus (1369-1415), a Czech theologian who lived roughly around the same time, advanced a form of *sola scriptura* by insisting that Scripture has primacy over the Magisterium and Church councils.

Protestants claim that the Bible teaches *sola scriptura* and that the doctrine goes back to Jesus. This claim amounts to an attempt to introduce the belief back into the pages of Scripture, in the process jumping over fourteen centuries of Church practice and belief. A review of historical continuity—or lack thereof—shows whether or not a belief originated with Jesus and the apostles or if it appeared later in time.

Let's look at some of the more popular passages that Protestants cite to establish *sola scriptura*'s ancient pedigree. It is beyond the scope of this book to conduct a systematic refutation of *sola scriptura* from a biblical perspective, but this list—and a Catholic response to the items in it—can get us to a working understanding of Protestant proof texts and how they fall flat.

1) Matthew 4:1–11: *"It is written . . ."*

Jesus is here being tempted in the desert by the devil. He responds to the devil three times by saying, "It is written . . ." and then quotes Scripture.

But Jesus is not quoting just any Scripture. In all three instances, he is quoting from Deuteronomy (8:3, 6:16, and 6:13), and these passages are specifically about the Israelites' experience *in the desert* when they were unfaithful to God and failed to trust him. Jesus was recalling the Israelites' failures so that he could demonstrate absolute trust in and fidelity to God where they did not.

In other words, in a decisive and particularly relevant blow to the devil, Jesus was redeeming and transforming the Israelites' failure. The underlying issue has nothing at all to do with *sola scriptura*, but rather with man's relationship to God. Jesus was demonstrating that he is the perfectly obedient Son, as the

Israelites *should* have been, and when the devil realizes he can't get Jesus to fail God, he departs.

2) Acts 17:10–11: *"The brethren immediately sent Paul and Silas away by night to Berea; and when they arrived they went into the Jewish synagogue. Now these Jews were more noble than those in Thessalonica, for they received the word with all eagerness, examining the scriptures daily to see if these things were so."*

It might look as though "Scripture alone" is the sole rule of faith for the Bereans. But it is important here to understand the broader context.

Paul was preaching in Thessalonica for three weeks and gaining converts in the process. But because some of those converts were coming from the synagogue where Paul was preaching, the Jews there were not pleased about losing members of their congregation and hence stirred up a commotion. They attempted to bring Paul and Silas before an assembly to accuse them of causing problems, but when they couldn't find these two at Jason's house, where they were staying, they instead dragged Jason and some other Christians before the city's magistrates. Word was sent to Paul and Silas that they were in danger, and so the Christians in Thessalonica had them leave the city under the cover of darkness and go to Berea. There, Paul went to another synagogue and preached about Jesus. But, as a counter to the aggressive response Paul experienced in Thessalonica, the Bereans received his message "with all eagerness."

So the Bereans were "more noble" not because they searched the scriptures, but because they did not treat Paul and Silas harshly, as the Thessalonians had. They were truly open-minded in the sense of being willing to consider what Paul was telling them. That is hardly a matter of supporting the idea that Scripture is the only infallible authority.

Furthermore, there are absolutely no Old Testament passages ("the scriptures" to which Paul was referring) that clearly state that "the Messiah had to suffer and die and rise from the dead on the third day." It is Paul's authoritative, apostolic teaching that "connected these dots" for the Bereans. But if *sola scriptura* were true, no examination and searching of the scriptures would have been necessary, because the teaching in question is *the central teaching of the Christian faith.*

But Acts 17 shows that this teaching was *not* sufficiently clear to the Thessalonians or the Bereans, who came to understand it only *after* Paul expounded on the Old Testament. If anything, this passage supports the Catholic position that Scripture is always coupled with official magisterial teaching.

3) 1 Corinthians 4:6: *"I have applied all this to myself and Apollos for your benefit, brethren, that you may learn by us not to go beyond what is written, that none of you may be puffed up in favor of one against another."*

Protestants are quick to emphasize the "not going beyond what is written" part, as Catholics allegedly do when they employ Sacred Tradition. A lot could be said about this verse, but consider at least the following.

The first Protestant leaders did not see this verse as helpful to their *sola scriptura* cause. None of them used this verse to establish the doctrine. John Calvin even said,

> The clause *above what is written* may be explained in two ways—either as referring to Paul's writings, or to the proofs from Scripture which he has brought

> forward. As this, however, is a matter of small moment, my readers may be left at liberty to take whichever they may prefer.[27]

If Calvin felt that this verse was "of small moment," whose interpretation was left to the reader's personal preference, clearly he did not intend it as a proof text for *sola scriptura*.

In this same letter, Paul explicitly affirms the believers in Corinth for having adhered to Sacred Tradition: "I commend you because you remember me in everything and maintain the traditions even as I have delivered them to you" (11:2). He is not going to advance one principle to the Corinthians in chapter four only to flatly contradict it in chapter eleven.

Bible scholars readily admit that the meaning of "what is written" is obscure, so how useful can this verse be to use in support of a central Protestant belief? If anything, Protestants would be guilty of *eisegesis*—reading something into the passage—instead of *exegesis*, pulling something out of the passage.

To give the reader some idea of the difficulties inherent in this verse, apologist Karlo Broussard offers the following possibilities[28] as to what is meant by "what is written":

- the scriptures in general concerning conduct for preachers;
- the Old Testament passages Paul already quoted in 1 Corinthians 1:19, 31; 2:16; 3:19-20;
- the metaphors of planting and building used in 1 Corinthians 3:15-17, the implication being that we should avoid false teachers who add to the gospel;

- more generally, to everything Paul himself wrote in the preceding chapters of the same epistle concerning Christian conduct;
- a Christian slogan or proverb used to address those causing discord in the community, a slogan that meant something akin to "keep within the rules"; or
- a public document for the Corinthian church that Paul modeled on cultic bylaws in order to lay out guidelines and principles necessary to preserve peace and prosperity.

The only clear thing seems to be that not going "beyond what is written" cannot possibly refer to *sola scriptura.*

4) 2 Timothy 3:16–17: *"All scripture is inspired by God and profitable for teaching, for reproof, for correction, and for training in righteousness, that the man of God may be complete, equipped for every good work."*

The Greek word *pasa*, which is often rendered as "all," actually means "every," and it "means 'all' in the sense of 'each (every) part that applies.'"[29] In other words, the Greek means that each and every "scripture" is profitable. If the doctrine of *sola scriptura* were true, then based on the Greek in verse 16, each and every book of the Bible could stand on its own as the sole rule of faith, which is obviously absurd. Just read Philemon or Jude, for example, and see how difficult it would be to construct an entire theological system based on either of these two short letters.

The "scripture" Paul is referring to is the Old Testament, made plain by his reference to it being known "from infancy" by Timothy. The New Testament did not yet exist (it was incomplete), so it simply could not have been part of Paul's understanding of what "scripture" referred to. This means that if we take his words at face value and in context, *sola scriptura* would mean that the Old Testament is the Christian's sole rule of faith. This is a premise that all Christians would rightly reject. The Old Testament was incomplete as a rule of faith until its full meaning was made known in the writings of the New Testament coupled with apostolic Tradition.

The Greek word *óphelimos* used in verse 16 means "useful" or "profitable," not "sufficient."[30] An example of this difference would be to say that water is useful for our existence (necessary!), but not sufficient. It is not the only thing we need to survive. We also need food, clothing, and shelter. In a similar way, Scripture is "useful" in the life of the believer, but it was never meant to be the only source of Christian teaching.

The Greek word *exartizo*, in verse 17, translated in the RSVCE as "equipped" (other Bible versions read something like "fully equipped" or "thoroughly furnished"), is claimed by Protestants as proof of *sola scriptura*, because this word implies that nothing else is needed for the "man of God." However, though the man of God may be "equipped," it does not guarantee a correct interpretation or application of any given Scripture passage. Being equipped and possessing knowledge and understanding of your equipment are not the same. The man of God must also be taught how to correctly use and interpret Scripture—just like how Paul taught Timothy—even though he may already be "equipped" with it.

5) Rev. 22:18-19: *"I warn every one who hears the words of the prophecy of this book: if any one adds to them, God will add to him the plagues described in this book, and if any one takes away from the* *words of the book of this prophecy, God will take away his share in the tree of life and in the holy city, which are described in this book."*

When John says that nothing is to be added to or taken from the "words of the prophecy of this book," he is not referring to Sacred Tradition being "added" to Sacred Scripture. The context shows that the "book" referred to here is only Revelation, not the whole Bible. We know this because John says that anyone who is guilty of adding to "this book" will be cursed with the plagues "written in this book"—namely, the ones he described earlier in Revelation. The Bible as we know it did not exist when this passage was written and therefore could not be what was meant.* Furthermore, the Greek word that John uses here is *bibliou*, a diminutive form of *biblion*, which is singular.31 Since the Bible is actually a collection of seventy-three books, it cannot be what is meant by a singular noun. Had John meant to refer to all seventy-three books, he would have needed the Greek plural noun, *biblia*—essentially meaning "these books."

The same warning not to add or subtract words is used in Deuteronomy 4:2, which reads, "You shall not add to the word which I command you, nor take from it; that you may keep the commandments of the LORD your God which I command

* "This list is the same as the one given in the Church's final, definitive, explicit, infallible declaration as to which books are to be included in the Bible, which was made by the Council of Trent, Session IV, in 1546. Earlier lists of canonical books were the list in the 'Decretal of Gelasius,' which was issued by authority of Pope Damasus in 382, and the canon of Pope St. Innocent I, which was sent to a Frankish bishop in 405. Neither document was intended to be an infallible statement binding the whole Church, but both documents include the same seventy-three books as the list of the Council of Trent in the mid-sixteenth century" (*The Catholic Encyclopedia* [New York: The Encyclopedia Press, 1913], Vol. 3, 272).

you." If we were to understand Revelation 22:18–19 the way Protestants suggest, then it proves too much, because anything in the Bible beyond the decrees of the Old Testament law would be non-canonical—including the New Testament! This prohibition against "adding," therefore, cannot serve to validate the doctrine of *sola scriptura*.

There are many other proof texts we could discuss, but these suffice for our purposes. That is to say, if *sola scriptura* cannot be found until over a thousand years after Jesus' earthly life, then the doctrine must lack the historical continuity intrinsic to apostolic teaching. Worse, in practice, we see that it initiated a radical break with the Christian past.

Some Protestants might object that at least some of the early Church Fathers *did* in fact teach *sola scriptura*, so the doctrine's origin goes back way before the Reformation. Take, for example, Nathan Busenitz, a Protestant pastor and seminary dean, who analyzes the Arian crisis like this:

> How did these early Christian leaders know that the doctrine they were defending was, in fact, a truth worth fighting for? How did they know they were right and the Arians were wrong? Was it on the basis of oral tradition, a previous church council, or an edict from the bishop of Rome? No. They ultimately defended the truth by appealing to the scriptures.[32]

Starting with Gregory of Nyssa, Busenitz quotes a passage from *Dogmatic Treatises* that says, "Let the inspired Scripture, then, be our umpire, and the vote of truth will surely be given to those whose dogmas are found to agree with the divine words." He then notes, "When Arian custom ran contrary to trinitarian custom, to what authority did Gregory appeal? The scriptures."[33]

But here is the problem: Arius *also* appealed to the scriptures! So Gregory had to be appealing to more than just the words of the Bible; he had to be advocating for *a magisterial interpretation* of them. Gregory and other orthodox Church leaders were promoting the Church's living memory—that is, the way it had always understood the scriptures, especially as they pertain to the Person of Christ. This is apostolic Tradition!

Whether during the Arian crisis or in our own day, the scriptures *alone* are insufficient to settle a controversy because both parties can appeal to them and arrive at opposite interpretations. What made the Church's position right and the Arian position wrong is that the former had the authoritative apostolic teaching ("custom") behind it, whereas the latter did not. So the final court of appeal can't be Scripture, or at least can't be *only* Scripture. It has to be Scripture *as interpreted by the Church's Magisterium.*

Questions to Ask:

1. If the doctrine of *sola scriptura* cannot be traced back in an unbroken line from the present day all the way back to the first century, what does this fact suggest about its origin and legitimacy?

2. If *sola scriptura* didn't appear for well more than a millennium after Jesus and the apostles, how can it be anything other than a man-made tradition?

3. What is the most convincing or compelling explanation a Protestant apologist can give for why *sola scriptura* is absent from the Church's historical record?

4. What historical, textual, or liturgical evidence is there that *sola scriptura* was believed and taught in *each century* of the Church's existence?

REASON 9

HERETICS BASED THEIR DOCTRINES ON THEIR INTERPRETATION OF SCRIPTURE

From the beginning, the Church's popes, theologians, and saints defended the Faith from heresy. Paul, for instance, wrote the following stern words:

> I am astonished that you are so quickly deserting him who called you in the grace of Christ and turning to a different gospel—not that there is another gospel, but there are some who trouble you and want to pervert the gospel of Christ. But even if we, or an angel from heaven, should preach to you a gospel contrary to that which we preached to you, let him be accursed. As we have said before, so now I say again, If any one is preaching to you a gospel contrary to that which you received, let him be accursed (Gal. 1:6–9).

The Catholic Church responded to heresies by convening councils and appealing to Rome—that is, to the pope—to settle doctrinal disputes. The pope also intervened when there were other disputes and potential schisms. For example, at the end of the first century, Pope Clement intervened in a controversy in the Corinthian church and ended a schism there. In the second century, Pope Victor threatened to excommunicate a large portion of the Church in Asia because they disputed the date for celebrating Easter (the *Quartodeciman* controversy).

There is, in fact, a long line of heresies in the Church's history, and the Magisterium, under the leadership of the pope, stood as the defender of the Faith when these doctrinal irregularities arose. Consider a few examples:

1) *Dynamic Monarchianism*, or *adoptionism*, which appeared in the later second century, was held by various groups who claimed to base their views on Scripture.[34] It stressed the belief that God is one and is the sole monarch or ruler of the universe and that Jesus is a man "endowed with special powers from God, and thus in a way adopted as God's Son." (On the contrary, Jesus is God's Son by nature, not by adoption.) Epiphanius, in his fourth-century catalogue of heresies called the *Panarion*, claimed that the belief originated in Rome with a man named Theodotus the Tanner. Pope Victor responded to his heresy by excommunicating him.

2) In the early third century, a priest named Sabellius denied that the Father, Son, and Holy Spirit are separate Persons in the Godhead. He was excommunicated by Pope Callistus I (c. 220) and condemned again by Pope Damasus in 382 at the Council of Rome, and his teachings were rejected at the ecumenical councils of Nicaea, Constantinople, Ephesus, and

Chalcedon, whose proceedings are ratified by the pope in order to be binding.

3) In the early fifth century, a British monk and theologian named Pelagius denied that humans inherit original sin from Adam and asserted that we can become righteous (perfected) on our own by following the instruction and example of the Christian community—seemingly apart from God's divine grace. Worse still is that for Pelagius, Jesus is no longer our Redeemer, but just a helpful exemplar for living a holy life. Pelagius was excommunicated by Pope Innocent I in 417; condemned by a local council of Carthage in 418; and condemned by the ecumenical council of Ephesus in 431, whose proceedings were ratified by Pope Celestine I.

4) Nestorius, the archbishop of Constantinople from 428 to 431, claimed that Jesus existed as two persons—the human being and the divine Son of God—rather than one divine Person with two natures joined in what theologians call the *hypostatic union*. He also attacked the belief that the Blessed Mother should be called the mother of God (Greek: *Theotokos*, "God-bearer") because of the one she bore in her womb. Shocked at this turn of events, Cyril of Alexandria wrote to Pope Celestine I, who condemned Nestorius's teaching on Mary. Nestorius dug in his heels, so the Council of Ephesus, presided over by the pope, opened in 431 to officially settle the matter. Nestorius's teachings were formally condemned, and he was deposed as bishop of Constantinople.

5) *Monophysitism* in the fifth century was an erroneous reaction to Nestorianism. It asserted that Jesus has only one nature—divine, into which his human nature is absorbed—in contrast

to orthodox teaching, which says he has two: human and divine. This heresy was condemned at the ecumenical council of Chalcedon in 451, whose proceedings were ratified by the pope's legates.

In each of these cases, we would expect Church leaders to have claimed that the pope was overstepping his authority *if* everyone understood that Scripture—not the pope, an ecumenical council, or anything else—is the only binding authority in the Church. Yet they didn't.

Protestant Objection: Other Church leaders *did* react against Pope Victor when he threatened excommunication. Eusebius, the third-century Church historian, wrote about this situation, and he notes that Pope Victor was "sharply rebuked."[35] So your claim is false.

Catholic Response: They reacted because they felt his punishment was too harsh, not because they thought he lacked the authority to impose it.

When heretics "go rogue," they defend their erroneous beliefs with their interpretations of Scripture, arrived at apart from Sacred Tradition and the Magisterium, the teaching office of the Church. In the case of Arius, the magisterial authority of the Church, with the pope at the top as the guarantor of the Faith, declared his interpretation faulty. Arius, according to his interpretation, disagreed. So who should have the final say? Or rather, who was given the authority to have the final say?

The pattern we see in these instances is that the heretic or the heretical teachings are formally condemned by Rome in one way or another—by the pope directly or indirectly through his legates, who ratified the proceedings of ecumenical councils.

Now let's consider Martin Luther. In resisting the pope and the Catholic Church, he promoted biblical interpretations based on his own self-imposed authority and in contradiction to what the Magisterium had taught. When Luther stood before John Eck, the speaker of the assembly at Worms (April 18, 1521) and an official of the archbishop of Trier, Eck aptly (and charitably) summed up Luther's approach to the Bible:

> Your plea to be heard from Scripture is the one always made by heretics. You do nothing but renew the errors of Wycliffe and Hus. How will the Jews, how will the Turks, exult to hear Christians discussing whether they have been wrong all these years!
>
> Martin, how can you assume that you are the only one to understand the sense of Scripture? Would you put your judgment above that of so many famous men and claim that you know more than they all? You have no right to call into question the most holy orthodox faith, instituted by Christ the perfect lawgiver, proclaimed throughout the world by the apostles, sealed by the red blood of the martyrs, confirmed by the sacred councils, defined by the Church in which all our fathers believed until death and gave to us as an inheritance, and which now we are forbidden by the pope and the emperor to discuss lest there be no end of debate.[36]

Richard von Greiffenklau, the archbishop of Trier, and John Cochlaeus, dean of the chapter-foundation of Our Lady at Frankfurt on the Main, also attempted to win Luther back to orthodoxy,[37] but Luther was not persuaded. He refused to recant his teachings, even though he asserted that a true Christian should be willing to be corrected:

> If you want to be saved and be a Christian, then stay open to correction. Preachers have to rebuke, or they should leave their position. The Christian who won't accept correction is only pretending to be a Christian.[38]

Yet Luther also made it clear that he didn't want to be told his beliefs were false and in opposition to what the Church had taught. When correction was offered to him, he spurned it with contempt. At this assembly, he explicitly rejected the authority of popes and Church councils, claiming instead that he was bound "by Scripture and plain reason" and his conscience.

It is evident that using the Bible alone cannot guarantee that you will arrive at doctrinal truth. The history of the Church and the numerous heresies[39] it has confronted testify as to what happens when *sola scriptura* is used as a rule of faith. Protestants seem to forget that one very important reason why Jesus established his Church was to *call out* heretical teachings and *reject them* as distortions of "the faith that was once for all handed down the holy ones" (Jude 1:3). If Protestantism is true, then Christ's Church instead fell prey to those heresies.

Questions to Ask:

1. How is Luther's approach to biblical interpretation different from the approach used by the heretics of the early Church and beyond?

2. Jesus put forth three doctrinal authorities for his Church: Scripture, Tradition, and the Magisterium. Luther rejected two of these—but on whose authority?

3. What do you say to someone who is shown to be wrong about something but insists on maintaining his error?

4. Why were Church councils and interventions by the pope necessary to combat heresies if Scripture alone is the Church's rule of faith?

REASON 10

THE CLAIM THAT SCRIPTURE IS "SELF-AUTHENTICATING" DOES NOT HOLD UP

Many Protestants subscribe to the idea that Scripture is "self-authenticating"—that is, the books of the Bible witness to themselves that they are inspired of God. A cursory examination of Church history will show how false this claim is.

For example, the canonical status of several New Testament books—James, Jude, 2 Peter, 2 John, 3 John, and Revelation—was disputed for some time. Before the Catholic Church settled the canon of Scripture, major theologians like Athanasius (297-373), Jerome (c. 342-420), and Augustine (354-430) drew up lists of New Testament books, but none of them exactly matched the New Testament canon that the Church established at the end of the fourth century, which we still use today.[40]

If the Bible were self-authenticating, then such disputes would not have happened, or at least it would not have taken hundreds of years to resolve them.

Where in Scripture do Protestants find their proof that the Bible is self-authenticating? They usually cite 2 Timothy 3:16: "All scripture, inspired of God, is profitable."* But if the claim that Scripture is inspired is *in Scripture*, is that enough? After all, Christian Scientists claim that Mary Baker Eddy's writings are inspired. Mormons claim the same about Joseph Smith's writings. Authors can make any claim about their own writings. But to ascertain if their writings actually are inspired, we need validation independent of those writings.

Before we can read 2 Timothy 3:16 (or Eddy or Smith) as a divinely inspired or "God-breathed" statement, an external agency that has the requisite authority to make such a determination must weigh in. This is the only way to avoid circular reasoning. Mary Baker Eddy's writing is "divinely inspired" because she says it is. Joseph Smith's, too. However, it is the Catholic Church that authenticated Paul's letter to Timothy as truly inspired by the Holy Spirit—and so now this verse really can be understood as being God's own statement about Scripture.

The difference separating Paul from Mary Baker Eddy and Joseph Smith is that whereas all three of them claim divine inspiration, only one of their claims was validated by an outside agency that Jesus invested with the requisite authority to make such a determination in the first place. Because such an important issue is at stake, when people ask, "Is this writing inspired?", they need a more reliable answer than, "Yes, because it says it is."

(Lest we get off-balance about whether the Catholic Church upholds the divine inspiration of Scripture, let me state unequivocally that it does. God the Holy Spirit is its primary author—see *Dei Verbum* 11.)

---

* The Greek word *theopneustos*, which is usually translated into English as "inspired," literally means "God-breathed."

Questions to Ask:

1. How can words on paper authenticate themselves? Or do they require a living human authenticator—and if so, whom?

2. Where does Scripture say it is self-authenticating?

3. Protestants say sixty-six books of the Bible are self-authenticating . . . but Catholics could say seventy-three books are self-authenticating. How do we resolve this problem?

4. If the scriptures are self-authenticating, why has there been so much disagreement and uncertainty over these books? Why has there been any disagreement at all?

5. If the scriptures are self-authenticating, why was the canon of the Bible not identified much earlier?

6. Why did the Catholic Church have to identify and then re-affirm the canon seven times before the Council of Trent?

REASON 11

NOT ONE OF THE ORIGINAL BIBLICAL MANUSCRIPTS EXISTS

Without original manuscripts, anyone who holds to *sola scriptura* cannot know for certain that he possesses the whole of Scripture. And so a sobering reality for Protestants is that when it comes to the Bible, there are no original manuscripts of *any* book!* There are thousands of *copies* of the originals—and copies of copies—but copies are not inspired.

But are the copies trustworthy? For Protestants to assess that, they have to rely on Bible scholars and historians and thus depend on something outside the Bible to establish the authenticity and accuracy of the manuscripts. Although these researchers can tell us things like the age of the manuscript, the writing

---

* The earliest copies of the Bible, *Codex Vaticanus* and *Codex Sinaiticus*, both date from the fourth century A.D. Neither one contains the entire Bible, as parts of the manuscripts have been lost or destroyed. The vast majority of the manuscripts that exist are copies of only portions of the Bible.

style of the author, and the meaning of idioms and symbols, this is nowhere near the same thing as telling us that what they are examining *is inspired Scripture*. A higher and more competent authority is required for that.

THE IRONY

The irony here is that it was due to the tireless efforts of Catholic monks working laboriously in their monasteries that the written word of God survived down through the centuries. The claim that the Catholic Church did everything in its power to suppress the Bible is a most pernicious falsehood, and it can readily be refuted by even the most basic examination of and research into Church history. Quite the contrary, the Catholic Church, in its unique role as guardian of the deposit of faith, protected the Bible's integrity from spurious and faulty translations, and it was these spurious and faulty copies of the Bible that it burned or destroyed to prevent false teachings from circulating.

Protestants may say that not having original biblical manuscripts is of no consequence because God preserved the Bible by safeguarding its duplication down through the centuries. However, there are two problems with this line of reasoning. The first is that the Bible does not explicitly state that God will providentially protect the transmission of manuscripts—and if it's not in Scripture, then it cannot be a rule of faith. Sure, you could point to a passage like 2 Timothy 3:14, or similar ones about passing on the Faith, but the problem for Protestants is that such verses establish the *oral* transmission of apostolic teaching, not the written transmission.

The second problem is that if you assert that God protected the *written* transmission of his word, then why can you not also assert that he did likewise with its *oral* transmission? Recall the twofold form of God's revelation mentioned in 2 Thessalonians 2:15. Remember that the preaching of the gospel and the apostolic teaching all began as an oral tradition (Luke 1:1-4, Rom. 10:17). It was not until later on that *some* of the oral tradition was put into writing—becoming Sacred Scripture—and it was later still that the Church declared these writings inspired and authoritative.

Protestant Objection: God *did* providentially protect the oral transmission of his word until such time as what was needed was written down and became Scripture. From that point on, there was no longer a need for the oral tradition.

Catholic Response: Your claim assumes several things, none of which is explicitly stated in Scripture:

- that the content of oral tradition would be replaced by written Scripture;
- that this process would not only take place, but be valid and binding upon Christians;
- that written content is inherently superior to oral content and therefore supersedes it;
- that what became inscripturated could somehow be identified as divine revelation without an external agency to vouch for and verify it; and

- that the part of oral tradition that was not written down became, for all intents and purposes, useless.

But if none of these assumptions is *in* Scripture—and none of the early Church Fathers attests to any of these things happening, either—then how can they be a part of *sola scriptura* . . . or defend it?

Protestants have an insurmountable problem. They cannot go back to the original manuscripts—what scholars call the *autographs*—*because they don't exist.* Protestants are compelled, therefore, to rely on other things, which necessarily violate *sola scriptura* because they go beyond the original biblical text.

- They can claim that copies (and copies of copies) of the autographs are divinely inspired.
- They can trust Bible scholars in their judgment about the integrity of the manuscripts we do have . . . but such scholars ultimately encounter the same problem of not being able to get to the original sources.
- In the case of an issue like the ending of Mark's Gospel, they can trust their "best guess." (See the next reason.)
- Or they can run the risk of adding to or deleting from the original manuscripts.

RELIABLE SCRIPTURE

Bible scholars maintain that there are exceedingly good reasons to trust the biblical text as we have it today. Compared to other works of antiquity, the Bible manuscripts far exceed their secular or historical counterparts both in number and proximity to the events they record. There are no legitimate reasons to cast any serious doubt on the biblical text as we have it, but unlike Protestants, Catholics comfortably maintain this position because it is framed by apostolic Tradition, the Church's Magisterium, and the Church's proclamation of the good news of Jesus Christ for 2,000 years.

Protestants, who have explicitly rejected these authorities, must necessarily rely on the institution they rebelled against for having not only created those manuscript copies, but also preserved them through the centuries along with other important Church documents. These thousands of biblical manuscripts existed long before Protestantism came into existence, and the Catholic Church identified the words they contain as inspired.

To be fair, Protestant Bible scholars also maintain that there are exceedingly good reasons to trust the biblical text as we have it today. However, they necessarily rely on the work of Catholics (especially monks) who tirelessly copied Bible manuscript after Bible manuscript.[41] Protestant Bible scholars have a wealth of material to work with thanks to Catholics, particularly where the New Testament is concerned.

Questions to Ask:

1. If God safeguarded the copying of the biblical text through time, which agency or organization did he use to do it?

2. On what basis do Protestants accept the inspired status of all the books in the Bible?

3. If copies of the original biblical manuscripts are not inspired, why should a Protestant trust the contents of the Bible that comprises those copies? Can the answer be based on the Bible alone, or must there be an appeal to something else?

4. How do Protestants know for sure that their Bibles contain all of the Scripture inspired by the Holy Spirit—no more and no less?

REASON 12

THE BIBLICAL MANUSCRIPTS CONTAIN MANY THOUSANDS OF VARIANTS

Within the thousands of biblical manuscripts in existence, there are many thousands of differences in the text, called *variants*. Raymond F. Collins, a Catholic priest and expert on the New Testament, and the author or editor of twenty books on the New Testament, estimates that there are over 200,000 variants.[43]

The vast majority of these variants split over minor concerns such as spelling, word order, word addition or deletion, and the like—what today we might call a typo. But there are also variants of a more important nature:

(a) Scribes sometimes modified the biblical texts to establish doctrinal correctness, to harmonize passages, and to accommodate them to historical fact.[44]

(b) There are some verses for which there are different manuscript readings, such as John 7:39, Acts 6:8, Colossians 2:2, and 1 Thessalonians 3:2.[45]

The Protestant now has to ask: *How do I know I have what the biblical authors originally wrote?* And if this is so, how can Protestants profess to base their beliefs solely on the Bible when they cannot determine the textual authenticity of the Bible, at least in some places?

TOUCHING DOCTRINE

It has been maintained by Protestants that in all the variations in biblical manuscripts, not one touches upon a major doctrine. Even though this assertion is untrue, it does not alter the fact that the Protestant is here admitting, at least obliquely, that it is permissible to accept something less than or different from the "real" Bible. And if this is true, then Protestants themselves have begun to undermine *sola scriptura*.

In some parts of the Bible, the differences among opposing variants are significant. Consider these two examples.

First, according to the manuscripts we have, there are four possible endings for Mark's Gospel:

1) the shorter ending, which includes verses 1-8 of chapter 16;
2) the longer ending, which includes verses 1-8 plus verses 9-20;
3) the intermediate ending, which includes two to three lines of text between verse 8 and the longer ending; and
4) the longer ending in expanded form, which includes several verses after verse 14 of the longer ending.[46]

The best we can say about these different endings is that we just do not know for certain where Mark's Gospel originally ended. Depending on which ending is in a Protestant Bible, the publisher runs the risk of adding verses to or omitting verses from the original text. Even if a given Protestant Bible includes all four endings along with explanatory footnotes, the reader still cannot be certain which of the four endings is genuine. If Scripture alone is the Christian's rule of faith, then this issue becomes critical, lest Protestants run the risk of having less than the complete Bible.

This has ramifications: not only does the longer ending in Mark contain doctrinal content less apparent in the shorter version of his Gospel—for example, Mark 16:16 explicitly says baptism is necessary for salvation, which some Protestants dispute—but now we are confronted with various groups of Protestants disagreeing over how much of the Gospel of Mark is in fact inspired Scripture. Who is right?

Unlike Protestants, Catholics can trust the Magisterium to tell them.[47] Protestants have to trust their Bible scholars' opinions and judgments. Granted, these scholars are informed and can make educated opinions and judgments, but they don't claim to speak on Christ's behalf.

Second, there is manuscript support for variant readings in some critical verses of the Bible, such as John 1:18, where there are two possible renderings.[48] Some Protestant Bibles, such as the King James Version, read like the Catholic Douay-Rheims Bible: "No man hath seen God at any time: the only begotten *Son* Who is in the bosom of the Father, he hath declared him." Others read like the New International Version: "No one has ever seen God, but *God* the One and Only, who is at the Father's side, has made him known." (I added italics to highlight the difference.) Both forms are substantiated by manuscripts, and biblical scholars thus rely on their educated judgment to determine which one they think is correct. The same situation occurs in Acts 20:28, where the manuscripts show that Paul could be talking about either the "church of the *Lord*" (Greek: *kuriou*) or the "church of *God*" (Greek: *theou*).[49]

This point may seem negligible at first. But if someone denies a certain Christian doctrine, like Jesus' divinity, and you are trying to defend that doctrine, it is going to be more difficult if your opponent can argue with you about the translation you're using and diminish the force of your argument by questioning its accuracy. This leaves you less able to defend a biblical doctrine—perhaps even a major doctrine!—and on the basis of *sola scriptura*, this is quite problematic.

Questions to Ask:

1. Where does Mark's Gospel end, and why does it matter to know?

2. Which ending for Mark's Gospel does *your* Bible translation have? Do you trust it? Why?

3. When you come to a Bible verse or passage whose reading is uncertain, how does *sola scriptura* apply?

4. Does it make sense to rely on Bible scholars for an authentic picture of the Bible, or would we do better to trust the teaching authority established by Christ?

REASON 13

THERE ARE THOUSANDS OF BIBLE VERSIONS

Not only are there thousands of *variants* among the manuscripts, but history has known thousands of Bible *versions*, too. Some versions are actually translations of translations, which can result in distortions from one language to the next.

SO MANY VERSIONS

According to www.bible.com/versions, there are about 3,200 versions of the Bible as of April 2024. As an indicator of how quickly Bible versions appear (or are discovered), when I first consulted this website in June 2020, it listed the total number at 2,090. About one month later, the total was 2,104.

Some translations are clearly inferior to others. Biblical research has made great progress via modern archeological discoveries that have significantly improved our knowledge of the ancient biblical languages and cultures. For example, the discovery of the Dead Sea Scrolls at Qumran (in modern-day Israel) starting in 1946 has been hailed as "the greatest archeological find of the twentieth century." The find consisted of more than 900 ancient manuscripts, 240 of which are of the Hebrew Bible (the Old Testament), written roughly between 250 B.C. and A.D. 68. The manuscripts shed light on the practices and beliefs of ancient Judaism (and thus on the world in which Jesus lived), which in turn sheds light on the early Christians and their writings. They also pushed back the date of our oldest complete Hebrew Bible (formerly the Leningrad Codex, 1008) by more than 900 years.

Thanks to the Dead Sea Scrolls, modern Bible versions are superior to older versions—directly for the Old Testament, and indirectly for the New Testament:

> The Dead Sea Scrolls help scholars get closer to the original OT texts where variants have entered the tradition, plus they help set the historical and cultural context for the Intertestamental and New Testament eras.

It may come as a surprise that the increase of biblical knowledge creates a problem for *sola scriptura*: it means that modern Protestants have a more accurate Bible, and thus a "more authoritative" final authority, than what their predecessors had. So how could *sola scriptura* have worked for Protestants operating before the discovery of the Dead Sea Scrolls? The final authority for their doctrines and beliefs, it turns out, was not final after all. An improved version came along and replaced it. And if this is true now, who is to say that there may not be another important archeological or manuscript find in the future that will render our current translations less accurate?

To illustrate how significant this issue can be, consider the following. The FAQ section of Biblica, The International Bible Society's web page, asks, "Why does the NIV [New International Version] omit or have missing verses?" The response given says in part,

> When comparing the NIV with the King James Version (KJV), it would seem that there are some verses "missing" in the NIV (and other trusted translations such as the CEV, CSB, ESV, GNB, HCSB, NET, NLT, etc.). Actually, that is not the case. . . .
>
> In the years since 1611, many older manuscripts have been discovered and carefully evaluated by scholars. Their conclusion is that the older manuscripts are more reliable. This has given modern translators unprecedented access to manuscripts much closer in time to the original documents. Therefore, translations such as the NIV actually reflect better Bible scholarship than was available in 1611 when the KJV was published.
>
> The verses or phrases that appeared in the KJV, but have been "omitted" in most trusted translations today, are not found in the oldest and most reliable manuscripts. Modern translators include or reference them in footnotes. These footnotes are intended to help the reader understand that certain perceived differences in the text are due to improved biblical scholarship. The treatment of these verses has not changed recently and reflects a consensus among the majority of Bible scholars.

The website affirms that modern manuscript discoveries have improved our biblical knowledge, effectively making, for instance, the NIV more authoritative than the KJV. But far more noteworthy is the admission that what once was a verse in the biblical text—that is, *inspired Scripture*—has since been removed and relegated to a footnote! In the process, it was "downgraded" from God's word to a *scholarly reference*.

Notwithstanding the gloss the article puts on the matter, it *is* "actually the case" that verses are now missing from what was until relatively recently the authoritative Protestant biblical text.

"But," a Protestant might object, "a similar thing happens with Catholic translations." To no avail, though, because the issue is of significantly less consequence for Catholics. Unlike a Protestant whose only source of authority is the Bible, Catholics have always had the Magisterium and Sacred Tradition to guide them. These authorities exist in part to guide us—*authoritatively*—to a proper understanding and interpretation of the Bible.

For Catholics, discrepancies and updates in Bible versions are resolved through the guidance of a teaching authority that speaks for Christ. Catholic bishops issue an *imprimatur* (meaning "let it be printed") to some Bible versions and other spiritual literature to assure the reader that the book contains nothing contrary to official Church teaching. So whether a given verse is listed in the biblical text or given as a footnote, Catholics can rest assured that the integrity of their beliefs has not been compromised. How could a *sola scriptura*-believing Protestant say the same?

Questions to Ask:

1. Jehovah's Witnesses (JW) use their own translation of the Bible, the *New World Translation*. Catholic and Protestant scholars alike consider it a distortion of the biblical text. But the Witnesses appeal to Bible scholars to support their renderings, just as mainline Protestants do. How do we resolve this problem, and how do we avoid it devolving into pitting one group of scholars against another?

2. If the Catholic Church as an institution translates the Bible to align with the beliefs of the millennia-old Catholic Church, it seems there's an argument to be made for that. But doesn't it look less reasonable if every individual Protestant is empowered to translate the scriptures according to his own individual, personal beliefs?

3. If God is guiding our understanding of the Bible apart from the Magisterium, why did he allow the Dead Sea Scrolls to be discovered so late? Shouldn't we have needed their help much sooner?

4. The NIV is more authoritative than the KJV because it is a more accurate translation. How should a Protestant view this difference and its impact on *sola scriptura*?

5. Can *sola scriptura* apply to an "inferior" version of the Bible? How can an "inferior" version of Scripture be the single rule of faith for a Christian—and how do we know we're not relying on such a version now?

REASON 14

FOR FOURTEEN CENTURIES, BELIEVERS ALMOST NEVER COULD OBTAIN A BIBLE

A key element of *sola scriptura* is the idea that the Holy Spirit will enlighten each believer unto the correct interpretation of Scripture. But for this doctrine to make sense, and for it to have any practical application, doesn't it stand to reason that each believer should own a Bible, or at least have access to one?

But the Bible was not mass-produced and readily available to individuals until the advent of the printing press in the fifteenth century. Even then, it would have taken quite some time for large numbers of Bibles to be printed and disseminated to the general population:

> The political systems, economies, logistical networks, and travel infrastructure that make the mass distribution of Bibles possible today simply did not exist for three quarters of Church history. There was no way to

> get the books to the peasants, and no way the peasants could have afforded them in the first place.[52]

It should be noted, by the way, that the inventor of the printing press, Johannes Gutenberg, was Catholic, and that the first book he printed was the Bible (c. 1455). The first printed Bible contained seventy-three books—the same number as in today's Catholic Bible, and the same number that the Catholic Church has invariably identified over the course of more than a millennium. Martin Luther deleted seven books from the Old Testament, after the canon had already been identified and after the Bible had already begun being printed.

Because of the lengthy amount of time during which mass-produced Bibles did not exist, for *sola scriptura* to work, millions and millions of Christians who lived prior to the fifteenth century would have to have been left without a final authority, unless by chance they had access to a hand-copied Bible. The likelihood of this is remote, since such copies were extremely expensive to make. If God were actually the author of the *sola scriptura* doctrine, then the means by which the fullness of his revelation in Christ would not be made readily available to the masses for fourteen centuries after Jesus walked the earth!

Questions to Ask:

1. If the first Bible to be printed contained the same number of books—seventy-three—that the Catholic Church had consistently identified on multiple occasions, why don't Protestant Bibles have seventy-three books also?

2. Why would God establish such an important doctrine as *sola scriptura* if it couldn't be put into practice until the fifteenth century or later?

3. How did people hear and know the scriptures for all those intervening centuries between the time of Christ and the apostles and the invention of the printing press? Is the answer to this question closer to the Protestant position or the Catholic position?

4. On whose authority did Martin Luther delete books from the Old Testament? (Yes, he had his *reasons* for doing so. I am asking where he got the *authority* to do so.)

5. Does removing books from the Bible violate the doctrine of *sola scriptura*?

6. Does removing books from the Bible violate the integrity of Scripture?

REASON 15

FOR A LONG TIME, BIBLES WERE BEYOND MOST PEOPLE'S MEANS

Prior to the invention of the printing press, the only way to reproduce the Bible was to copy it by hand. This was an enormously expensive undertaking, and hence the vast majority of people could not afford to own a Bible. Biblica (also The International Bible Society), a Protestant organization, notes,

> Because of the huge size of complete Bibles, they were divided into several volumes, and each was very costly. Only the rich and the universities could afford them.[53]

CODEX SINAITICUS

"*Codex Sinaiticus*, a manuscript of the Christian Bible written in the middle of the fourth century, contains the earliest complete copy of the Christian New Testament. The handwritten text is in Greek. The

New Testament appears in the original vernacular language (koine) and the Old Testament in the version, known as the *Septuagint*, that was adopted by early Greek-speaking Christians."[54]

To put the issue in perspective:

> A manuscript containing a group of New Testament writings in the average format (about 200–250 folios of approximately 25 x 19 cm.) required the hides of at least fifty to sixty sheep or goats. This would mean quite a good size flock. Manuscripts would often need to be larger to accommodate more than a single group of writings, and this would require a greater number of hides.
>
> Only by considering this aspect can we gain some idea of what a manuscript of the New Testament would have cost in past centuries. For a larger manuscript (*Codex Sinaiticus* was originally at least 43 x 38 cm. in size) or one of a particularly fine quality of parchment, the expense would have multiplied.
>
> In fact, a manuscript of the New Testament represented a small fortune because the preparation of the parchment was only the first step. Once it had been prepared there was still the writing of the text to be done, as well as the illumination of the initials, and frequently also the addition of miniatures by an artist. When the parchment was stained with purple and inscribed with silver and gold lettering (and several such manuscripts have survived from the sixth century), clearly the manuscript must have

> been commissioned by persons of the upper class who could afford to ignore the expense.[55]

Even an individual priest, whom you might reasonably expect to have a Bible in his possession, would find himself facing a serious financial obstacle. In the latter part of the sixteenth century, a Bible would cost the equivalent of ten years of the average priest's income.[56]

How could most people be expected to decide doctrine for themselves if they couldn't afford the resource they needed to do that? I suppose people could have asked a rich person who owned a Bible if they could borrow it (very doubtful), and sure, people could perhaps have traveled to a university, where they might consult the sacred word (also doubtful). Practically speaking, these things were rather unlikely to happen for the average peasant.

What about individual Christians seeking to own only the New Testament, or even just a portion of it? Even here, the cost is beyond the means of the average person. The Protestant website Bible.org lists the following rounded costs to produce ancient manuscripts.[57] The unit of payment is the *denarius*, a standard silver coin that was the daily wage in the ancient Roman Empire for average, unskilled laborers and common soldiers (see Matt. 20:2 and John 12:5).

- 2,600 for Matthew
- 1,600 for Mark
- 2,800 for Luke
- 2,300 for John

These costs put ownership of even just one Gospel way beyond the means of the average person.

> In no way could an average Christian afford a New Testament, not to mention one Gospel. He might be able to afford a small epistle, if he scrimped and saved money, but the cost of daily living would typically prove too high.[58]

If we modernize these numbers, based on a five-day work week with an average of 4.3 weeks per month, totaling 21.5 days of work per month, it would take 121 months' worth of wages for Matthew, 74 months for Mark, 130 months for Luke, and 107 months for John. That's roughly ten years for Matthew, six years for Mark, eleven years for Luke, and nine years for John!

Bible.org also quotes from the fourth edition of *The Text of the New Testament: Its Transmission, Corruption, and Restoration*, by Bruce Metzger and Bart Ehrman, which states that the cost of producing a complete Bible like the *Codex Sinaiticus* would have come to about 30,000 denarii. This mind-blowing sum represents *120 years* of work for one person, based on our modern work week of five days, with two weeks off for vacation (i.e., fifty weeks of work per year at five days per week makes 250 work days). Even if we adjusted our work week to a suffocating seven days a week, fifty-two weeks a year, it would still take eighty-two years to earn 30,000 denarii.

FIRST PRINTINGS

"By studying the size of Gutenberg's paper supply, historians have estimated that he produced around 180 copies of his Bible during the early 1450s. That may seem minuscule, but at the time there were probably only around 30,000 books in all of Europe." (See Andrews, "7 Things You May Not Know," note 60.)

Perhaps people could have pooled their money to have a Bible made for them, but even then, the number needed to make the project affordable for all would be substantial—and hence unlikely. With the number of people needed to make the purchase possible, regulating its possession would have been a daunting task. Even if they agreed to take turns, how long could each person possibly have it, and how long until it came around again?

Let's be charitable and assume that these people agree to keep their Bible in a common location for access by all owners. You still end up having more or less the same problem: how often can any one person actually be able to spend time reading it while others are waiting to do the same?

Even when Johannes Gutenberg invented the printing press in the mid-fifteenth century, the cost of a Bible did not suddenly come within reach of the average person. Because they were still relatively few in number, they were a highly valued commodity—which *drove up* the price, based on the simple economic dynamics of supply and demand:

> Thanks to their obvious quality, the Bibles all sold before Gutenberg and Fust had even finished printing them. Some copies supposedly went for around thirty florins—an enormous sum at the time.[59]

I would add that the cost of producing a Bible is what gave rise to the practice of chaining them to a fixed location in a church or monastery. Some Protestants claim that the Catholic

Church did so to prevent the average believer from having access to the Bible, but the exact opposite is true. The Bible was chained to ensure that people who went to the church or monastery had access to it. Otherwise, it would be vulnerable to theft.

> With the appearance of cathedral schools and a dynamic mercantile class that sought both education and entertainment in reading, books were more sought after than ever before. It followed that books, both plain and fancy, were prime targets for thieves, whether criminals who broke into a library or impoverished students who could not resist pilfering and selling titles from the libraries they patronized. A library's most used books were not only chained to desks and lecterns to prevent theft, but often protected by a "book curse" to scourge whoever damaged or stole them.[60]

Those of us who were born prior to the advent of cell phones recall going to a phone booth to make a call. There you would find a phone directory secured to the booth with a cable or small chain—and for the same reason Bibles were chained. The phone company wanted its customers to have access to it, and had it not been secured to the booth, a thief or vandal could have easily walked off with it.

Questions to Ask:

1. Was the Bible for many centuries meant only for those who could afford a copy? Did God favor the rich?

2. Why would God establish a major doctrine by which most people for a long time would not have access to the exact thing they needed to put the doctrine into practice?

3. Even the invention of Gutenberg's printing press was not an immediate solution to the problem of Bible production. What impact does this reality have on the doctrine of *sola scriptura*?

4. In the absence of a Bible, how did people through the centuries hear the gospel and learn the doctrines Christ wanted them to believe? Is the answer to this question closer to the Protestant position or the Catholic position?

REASON 16

IT TOOK A LONG TIME TO MAKE A BIBLE

For 1,400 years after Jesus' time, the Bible was copied by hand. As you might imagine, this was a laborious and time-consuming process:

> In the Middle Ages, every book was made by hand. Each component required several tedious tasks, from carefully cutting sheets of parchment to writing the script, binding the pages, and protecting them with a cover. The scribe's duties were especially demanding, requiring meticulous care and long hours.[61]

This passage doesn't detail the process by which parchment—made from calf, goat, or sheep skin—was prepared for writing. This preparation was also quite time-consuming:

> The manufacture of parchment is quite involved. After the skin is removed from the animal and any hair or flesh is cleaned away, it is stretched on a wooden frame. While it is stretched, the parchment maker or *parchminer* scrapes the surface of the skin with a special curved knife. In order to create tension in the skin, scraping is alternated by wetting and drying the skin. The parchment is scraped, wetted, and dried several times to bring it to the right thickness and tautness. Sometimes a final finish is achieved using pumice as an abrasive followed by chalk in order to prepare the surface of the skin to accept ink.[62]

Metzger observed,

> Copying is also long, tedious work. It would take a scribe several months to copy just one Gospel. In some secular Greek manuscripts, scribes left a note at the end that indicates the patient labor involved: "As the traveler rejoices to see the home country, so the scribe rejoices to see the end of a manuscript!"[63]

If it took several months to copy just one Gospel, you may wonder how much time was needed to copy the whole Bible. Depending on your source, it was between twelve and fifteen months![64]

In addition to the parchment preparation and the copying, which were already phenomenally time-consuming, there were other considerations that added to the amount of time needed:

> Past the physical pen-to-parchment copying of the text, the rest of the book production process was

> equally difficult and specialized. Scribes, illustrators, and book binders would often be separate in their professions, because of the level of skill and amount of time needed to adequately perform each part of the process. The scribe would copy a text, then hand it off to the illustrator (if there even were illustrations, usually only seen in later manuscripts), and then it would be given to a binder to be sewn together at last. This process took copious amounts of time as well, not just because the tasks in themselves are time-consuming, but the book also may have had to travel to different monasteries or workshops in order for illuminations or bindings to be completed.[65]

The doctrine of *sola scriptura* would have subjected individual believers to a process that, because of the time involved in producing Bibles, restricted their access to a Bible in a major way. Essentially, the demand would far exceed the supply, leaving Protestants unable to implement one of their core doctrines.

Nor does this practical problem have to be restricted to the distant past. Bookstores the world over may have shelves full of Bibles, and the internet offers thousands of Bible translations for free, but not everyone in the world has access to a bookstore or a computer. Even in modern times, if *sola scriptura* is the sole rule of faith for a Christian, these people are flat out of luck.

But God knew in advance about the time-consuming nature of the copying process, just as he knows now about the uneven distribution of resources and access to media. It stands to plain reason that he would not have imposed such a critical doctrine as *sola scriptura*, knowing full well that the mechanisms by which it would have to be implemented would prevent it from coming about.

Questions to Ask:

1. If *sola scriptura* were true, why would God establish a major doctrine that would have to wait until the invention of the printing press to be implemented in a meaningful and productive way? Why would God leave his people in scriptural darkness for all those centuries?

2. For 1,400 years, who copied all the biblical manuscripts?

3. In the absence of readily available Bibles, what divinely appointed authority was in place to give the faithful the scriptural and moral guidance they needed?

REASON 17

EARLY NEW TESTAMENT MANUSCRIPTS WERE WRITTEN IN RUNNING HAND

The Greek manuscripts of the New Testament are divided into two main categories: *majuscules* (*uncials*) and *minuscules*. The former were written in even, capital letters; the latter were written in smaller, cursive script.

The text was also written in *running script*:

> In parchments from the fourth to the ninth centuries, both majuscules and minuscules were used for New Testament manuscripts, but by the eleventh century all the manuscripts were minuscules. In these early New Testament manuscripts, there were no spaces between either letters or words, rarely an indication that a word was "hyphenated," no chapter or verse divisions, no punctuation, and no accents or breathing marks on the Greek words. There was only a continuous flow of letters.[66]

To illustrate the ramifications of this kind of writing, imagine if the following letters were found in a biblical manuscript: GODISNOWHERE. There are two ways to render the spacing in English, and the theological difference between them is enormous:

GOD IS NOWHERE
GOD IS NOW HERE

What if the text itself is insufficient to establish where the spacing should go? We need something extra to guide us, lest we end up distorting what the author originally wrote.

You can see, then, why ancient biblical manuscripts had to be read with particular care. Even something as simple and seemingly harmless as a comma could end up causing a doctrinal dilemma.

For example, when Jesus is hanging on the cross, the "good thief" says to him, "Jesus, remember me when you come in your kingly power" (Luke 23:42). Jesus responds by saying, "Truly, I say to you, today you will be with me in Paradise" (v. 43). For a modern reader, the meaning of Jesus' words is easy to decipher because of the punctuation used.

In the New World Translation used by Jehovah's Witnesses, however, although the words of Luke 23:43 are translated essentially the same, the punctuation is different. Because the Witnesses do not believe that there is a particular judgment for people at the moment of their death, followed by a corresponding experience of heaven or hell, they move the comma so it bolsters their erroneous theology of what happens after death: that the person will remain in "soul sleep" until the resurrection.

Notice how this verse is rendered in these Catholic Bible versions:

- "Amen, I say to you, today you will be with me in Paradise" (New American Bible).
- "And he said to him, 'Truly, I say to you, today you will be with me in Paradise'" (Revised Standard Version, Catholic Edition).
- "And Jesus said to him: Amen I say to thee, this day thou shalt be with me in paradise" (Douay-Rheims Version).
- "'Indeed, I promise you,' he replied, 'today you will be with me in paradise'" (Jerusalem Bible).
- "He answered him, 'In truth I tell you, today you will be with me in paradise'" (New Jerusalem Bible).

Now compare these renderings to the New World Translation. Notice where the comma is placed relative to the word "today":

- "And he said to him: 'Truly I tell you today, you will be with me in paradise.'"[67]

LUKE 23:43, NWT

This verse is rendered the same way in Jehovah's Witnesses' 2013 Revision and 1984 Edition. The latter has a footnote at this verse: "'Today.' Although WH [Westcott and Hort] put a comma in the Gr. text before the word for 'today,' commas were not used in Gr. uncial mss. In keeping with the context, we omit the comma before 'today.' Sy^{c} (fifth cent. C.E.) renders this text: 'Amen, I say to thee to-day that with me thou shalt be in the Garden of Eden.'— F. C. Burkitt, *The Curetonian Version of the Four Gospels,* Vol. I, Cambridge, 1904."

This footnote illustrates two things. First, notice their comment: "In keeping with the context . . ." But whose context? Second, the Watch Tower Society also supports its translations with scholarship, as I have noted elsewhere. The question becomes whether its scholars are in line with "the faith which was once for all delivered to the saints" (Jude 1:3).

The shift is subtle but theologically significant. In Catholic translations, Jesus promises the good thief he will be in paradise *today*. In the NWT, moving the comma amounts to Jesus promising the good thief *today* that at some *future point* he will be in paradise—but *not* right after his death. In Catholic translations, being in paradise happens today; in the NWT, the *telling* happens today.

Since the early manuscripts did not use punctuation, how was the translator to know where to place the comma? On such an important doctrine as what happens to someone after death, the comma's placement becomes an issue. The only way to reflect authentic Christian teaching is to consult an authority outside the text. In this case, Catholics have such an authority: the Church's Magisterium. The only way for Protestants to know where the comma should be placed is to rely on the teachings already set forth by the Catholic Church.

In fairness, major Protestant translations render this verse as do the Catholic versions, placing the comma before "today" and not after. But without the guidance of the Catholic Magisterium on this doctrine, how can Protestants avoid admitting that the NWT rendering could be just as valid? And so an important doctrine is compromised because it's unclear when the good thief was with Jesus.

If the Jehovah's Witnesses were correct, then the interpretation of other passages in Scripture dealing with death and the afterlife would have to be reconsidered, because Scripture cannot contradict Scripture. Do we then end up with a doctrinal domino effect? For example, Paul writes in 2 Corinthians 5:8 that "we are confident, and have a good will to be absent rather from the body, and to be present with the Lord." He is saying that once we die, we go to be with the Lord. This is in harmony with Luke 23:43. But the Jehovah's Witnesses effectively assert, "Paul doesn't indicate *when* the person will go home to the Lord after dying. Hence, we believe there is an interim period between leaving the body and being with the Lord." You end up with dueling interpretations if all you have is Scripture verses to sling back and forth.

If *sola scriptura* were true, and if a Christian is even marginally less able to substantiate or defend an important doctrine on the basis of a translation issue that cannot be resolved by the text alone, then *sola scriptura* fails at the purpose for which Protestants claim it is designed.

Protestant Objection: We can resolve this issue by comparing Scripture with Scripture. We simply look at other passages that address death and the afterlife and apply their meaning to this passage.

Catholic Response: But how do you know that those other passages shed light on Luke 23:43 rather than the other way around? Or what about a verse like 2 Corinthians 5:8, which Jehovah's Witnesses can also distort to conform with their take on Luke 23:43?

Questions to Ask:

1. Why do you trust and accept where the comma is placed at Luke 23:43 in your particular translation of the New Testament?

2. On what basis do you tell a Jehovah's Witness that the NWT is in error in its placement of the comma in Luke 23:43? If you cite other Bible passages to support your interpretation, the Jehovah's Witness will do the same for his interpretation. Now what?

REASON 18

SOLA SCRIPTURA DEPENDS ON PEOPLE'S ABILITY TO READ

It is difficult to know global literacy rates since the first century with certainty, because there is no census from which to get the numbers. Literacy depended on any number of factors, including predominant languages or dialects, social class, and geography. However, I think two points could reasonably be made: literacy rates were much lower in more ancient times compared to today, and literacy didn't improve in a meaningful way until the advent of the printing press in the fifteenth century, when books started to be produced on a larger scale. Even then, it took time for books to be widely distributed and become affordable.

Philip Hughes, in *A Popular History of the Reformation*, notes that

> at the time when the great changes of the sixteenth century began, the mass of the people of western

> Europe could neither read nor write—perhaps as many as two out of three were completely illiterate.[69]

Another source[70] notes that in 1820, "only one in ten people in the world could read and write," and it puts the literacy rate in Europe starting in 1475 at under 20 percent. It also notes that although there was a fairly sharp increase from 1600 to 1700, European literacy rates were still in the 22- to 35-percent range by 1700.

What are we to make of these statistics? The point is that illiteracy was widespread until more recent times—say, in the last two centuries or so. What this means for *sola scriptura* is that in practice, even *if* the average person had access to a Bible—which we have already seen is highly improbable—the likelihood that he could read it was remote. And if literacy rates didn't improve substantially until the printing press was available or even later—until the Age of Enlightenment, as some researchers suggest, which didn't start until the late seventeenth century at the earliest (some historians put its start in the early eighteenth century)—it means that there was a huge gap in time when believers were effectively left without a Bible.

From a practical point of view, *sola scriptura* just *doesn't work* because the tools, resources, and abilities needed for it to function were not available to significant numbers of people for a significant stretch of time. Modern Protestant apologists defend the doctrine without accounting for these practical problems.

Questions to Ask:

1. Why does Jesus so consistently emphasize to his apostles the preaching and teaching of the good news, as opposed to allowing people to read Scripture for themselves?

2. Is there any unequivocal passage in the New Testament that concerns writing down God's word for general distribution?

3. Why would God have created a major doctrine that could not be utilized by most people for most of the Church's existence, and still can't be utilized by many today?

4. If you couldn't read, how useful was it to own or have access to a Bible?

REASON 19

UNDERSTANDING THE BIBLE INVOLVES MORE THAN JUST READING THE TEXT

The Bible was written roughly 2,000 to 3,300 years ago,* in three ancient languages, and using the idioms, symbols, and characteristic styles of writing that were indigenous to the cultures of those times. It would be naïve to assume that by merely reading the biblical text at face value, a person would *necessarily* arrive at a proper understanding of its meaning. At least, in the absence of a working knowledge of these literary considerations, the reader is unable to fully appreciate the richness of God's word. This is precisely why the Second Vatican Council stated,

---

* Scholarly estimates vary on when the Old Testament began to be written. Some say as early as about 1500 B.C. and others as late at about 1000 B.C. I have used a date that is roughly in between.

> To search out the intention of the sacred writers, attention should be given, among other things, to "literary norms." For truth is set forth and expressed differently in texts that are variously historical, prophetic, poetic, or of other forms of discourse. The interpreter must investigate what meaning the sacred writer intended to express and actually expressed in particular circumstances by using contemporary literary forms in accordance with the situation of his own time and culture.
>
> For the correct understanding of what the sacred author wanted to assert, due attention must be paid to the customary and characteristic styles of feeling, speaking, and narrating which prevailed at the time of the sacred writer, and to the patterns men normally employed at the period in their everyday dealings with one another (*Dei Verbum* 12).

The doctrine of *sola scriptura* seems to assume that anyone who picks up a Bible and reads it has a sufficient command of these literary considerations—that is, he understands ancient modes of writing; the historical contexts in which the writing was created; the use of symbols, imagery, and idioms of entirely foreign and temporally distant cultures; and the modes of typical, daily interactions of ancient people.

This is an enormous—and patently unreasonable—assumption. Let's take two examples of what happens when the reader is uneducated in these literary considerations.

Our first example is in John 2, at the wedding at Cana, where Jesus performs his first miracle and establishes his divine identity. As John puts it, "this, the first of his signs, Jesus did at Cana in

Galilee, and manifested his glory" (v. 11). It is a hugely important event in salvation history.

Mary, naturally, plays a significant role in this event by proactively approaching her son about a problem that has arisen and directing the servers to "do whatever he tells you" (v. 5). One verse prior, there is a brief interaction between Jesus and his mother in which Jesus says to her, after she has told him that the host has run short of wine, "O woman, what have you to do with me?"

Other translations read as follows:

- "'Woman, why do you involve me?' Jesus replied" (New International Version).
- "And Jesus said to her, 'Woman, what does that have to do with us?'" (New American Standard Bible).
- "Jesus said to her, 'Woman, what does your concern have to do with me?'" (New King James Version).

What we have here is a Semitic idiom rendered in Greek,[71] the language of the New Testament. In these versions, the idiom is rendered in a way that sounds as though Mary is almost pestering Jesus with her request. Some translations render the idiom in even harsher tones, resulting in an obscuring of what is happening between Jesus and Mary:

- "Dear woman, that's not our problem" (New Living Translation).
- "'You must not tell me what to do,' Jesus replied" (Good News Translation).

Of course, Jesus would *never* disrespect his mother, and he would *never* blithely or callously dismiss her concern. The *Catholic Encyclopedia*, for instance, notes,

> The Greek *ti emoi kai soi, gynai* is translated in the Vulgate, "Quid mihi et tibi est mulier?" In most English Catholic Bibles this is rendered, "Woman, what is it to me and to thee?" The translation adopted in the Authorized and Revised Versions, "Woman, what have I to do with thee?", even if better idiomatically, *conveys a wrong impression, for it gives the idea of a rebuke which is totally against the context.*[72]

There is a critical theological consideration here that the average reader may not know about based on the way the verse is translated and in the absence of a working understanding of Semitic idioms. The expression used here, which literally translates "what to me and to you,"[73] is better rendered in English as "What is this between you and me?"[74] The Douay-Rheims Bible hits closer to the mark on this verse: "And Jesus saith to her: Woman, what is that to me and to thee?"

Jesus is effectively saying to his mother, "What are the implications for you and for me if I grant your request? Do you understand the ultimate consequences of what you are asking?" What Jesus means is that once he performs this first miracle and thus publicly "announces" who he is, the clock begins ticking to where his ministry will lead: the cross. Jesus is really asking Mary, "Do you understand that if I perform this miracle, I begin walking the path to my cross, and you begin walking the path to your heart being pierced with a sword?" (Luke 2:35). This miracle ends with what John consistently refers to as Jesus' "hour"—the appointed time of his suffering, death, resurrection, and ascension.

Another theologically important aspect of this verse that probably gets lost without background knowledge is Jesus' use of the word *woman*. To modern American ears, the word smacks of disrespect because any son in his right mind would never refer to his mother this way—in *our* culture. But John is always purposeful about his word choice, and so we can assume that there is a deeper level of meaning here to be uncovered.

John specifically uses the word "woman" because he is drawing the reader's attention to another "woman" who was theologically significant: Eve. In Catholic theology, the first "woman" (Eve) lost fellowship with God through her disobedience and brought about sin, death, and a rupturing of her (and our) relationship with God. The second "woman" (Mary), through her obedience to God, brought about grace and new spiritual life as well as the restoration of our fellowship with God the Father through her son.

Based on the kinds of translations I cited above, how could a person possibly derive these meanings from the verse? In one case, Jesus seems to be annoyed at his mother, and in another, he is asking her a question with profound implications for both of them. In one case, Jesus seems to disrespect his mother, and in another, he makes an important theological connection. These understandings are universes apart, and the gaping disparity between them is the inevitable result of a failure to understand the idiom John is using.

Our second example is something Jesus says from the cross: "My God, my God, why hast thou forsaken me?" (Matt. 27:46). If you read and understand his words at face value, you could easily come away from the passage thinking that Jesus was despairing on the cross and felt that his Father had abandoned him.* But in fact, he is quoting the opening line of Psalm 22. It borders on blasphemy to suggest that the Father could ever abandon the Son, but without additional knowledge of Jewish practices in Jesus' day, you could end up entirely misreading the passage.

What Jewish practices? In Jesus' day, it was a common practice to recall a psalm by reciting just its opening verse. Look at Psalm 22, and you will see that it is divided into two parts: lament (vv. 1-21) and praise (vv. 22-32). The shift in tone from the first part to the second is dramatic. Whereas the psalm begins on a negative note—God is far away, he doesn't hear cries of anguish, he does not answer the man's call—it ends on a note of hope in God and praise of him.

Especially relevant here is verse 25, which emphasizes that God has *not* turned away from the innocent man in the psalm, who is pouring out his heart to God in an act of faith.

So when Jesus cries out, "My God, my God," he is calling to mind the entire psalm, not just the first line of it. Hence, what appears to be a cry of despair is actually a statement of faithful trust in God. A merely surface-level or literal reading of his words on the cross could be misconstrued to mean exactly the opposite of what they are intended to mean, and the reader would get entirely the wrong idea.

Protestants might respond by saying that this kind of problem is easily solved by readers having at their disposal various Bible study aids: lexicons, commentaries, dictionaries, and sermons. But these resources are a relatively modern thing, and they were unavailable to the general public for a long period of time. Moreover, doesn't the need for concordances, etc. imply that "the Bible alone" is not all the believer needs? Without

---

* I do not deny that in his humanity, Jesus may have felt something like despair. But in his divinity, Jesus was *always* united with his Father.

other resources or additional knowledge in these instances, the reader will miss the point the biblical writer intended. And then what are these extrabiblical resources if not a Protestant substitute for the Church's Magisterium?

Anyone who picks up a Bible and reads it will benefit by doing so. God's word is "living and active, sharper than any two-edged sword, piercing to the division of soul and spirit, of joints and marrow, and discerning the thoughts and intentions of the heart" (Heb. 4:12). But to divorce Scripture from the human contexts in which it arose—language and culture—and not to account for them minimizes Scripture's impact and puts the reader at a fundamental disadvantage. It robs him of the ability to plumb the meaning and riches of the word, like what we saw in our two examples. From the perspective of *sola scriptura*, this is quite problematic.

If Protestants object and assert that this kind of difficulty is nothing more than a translation issue, then we are right back to other inherent problems with "the Bible alone" discussed above. Besides, not every Bible version comes with explanatory notes to help the reader avoid such misunderstandings. Moreover, difficulties with interpretations and understandings are addressed by having magisterial guidance, which is precisely what Jesus set up in the first place with his Church's teaching authority to stand beside the scriptures.

Questions to Ask:

1. If you come across a Bible passage that you don't entirely understand, where do you turn for help in interpreting it? Why do you turn to this particular source? What makes it trustworthy?

2. Have you ever vetted the credentials of authors of the Bible resources you use? Are these authors connected in an unbroken chain to the living memory and teachings of the Church?

3. Would you ever counsel a fellow believer to read Scripture without the use of any kind of resource or aid?

4. How does your Bible translate the words between Jesus and Mary in John 2? Does your translation emphasize or obscure the actual meaning of this dialogue?

5. Has this section given you a new understanding of Jesus quoting Psalm 22 from the cross? What other Bible passages might you be misinterpreting?

REASON 20

SOLA SCRIPTURA CAN'T PROTECT AGAINST BAD BIBLE TRANSLATIONS

Another vital consideration is the reality that some versions of the Bible are outright perversions of the biblical text, as is the case with the Jehovah's Witnesses' New World Translation, mentioned above. Here the "translators" distort key passages in a way suited to their erroneous doctrines. Of the numerous examples I could cite, here are a few to illustrate the point. Note that in some instances, the "translators" are not *translating*, but *interpreting* the biblical text.

ABOUT THOSE TRANSLATORS

I say "translators" (with quotation marks) because of the four men who served on the New World Translation Committee, three of them had no formal education in the biblical languages. One member, Fred Franz, studied Greek for two years at the University of Cincinnati and was self-taught in Hebrew (Raymond Franz, *Crisis of Conscience: The Struggle Between Loyalty to God and Loyalty to One's Religion*, fourth edition, Atlanta: Commentary Press, 2002, 56, footnote 16).

The Watch Tower Society, the parent organization of the Jehovah's Witnesses, won't even disclose the names and credentials of the Translation Committee members because they wanted to remain anonymous, even after their deaths. They claimed that they wanted all the glory for their work to go to "Jehovah" and that their work should stand on its own merits (see *The Watchtower*, December 15, 1974, 767-768). Of course, this anonymity conveniently prevents anyone from uncovering the credentials of the committee members.

- In Genesis 1:2, God's "active force" is moving over the waters of creation, because Jehovah's Witnesses don't believe in the Trinity or in the Holy Spirit as a divine person. The Holy Spirit is always rendered in the NWT as "active force" or "holy spirit," without the capital letters that normally denote divinity and personhood.
- In Matthew 26:26, Jesus says, "This means my body" instead of "This is my body" because Witnesses deny the Real Presence of Christ in the Eucharist.
- In Matthew 27:32, Simon of Cyrene carries Jesus' "torture stake" because Witnesses deny that Jesus was crucified on a cross. See the entire chapter, where the Greek words for "crucified" and "cross" are rendered as "nailed to the stake" or "executed on the stake" and "torture stake."
- In Matthew 2:2 and 28:9 (and other places), where people worship Jesus, the Greek word for worship (*proskuneō*) is rendered as "do obeisance" because

Jehovah's Witnesses can't have Jesus being worshiped. Worship is a prerogative that belongs exclusively to God, and since Witnesses reject Jesus' divinity, they downgrade worship of Jesus to honor and respect.

- In John 1:1, the prologue reads, "And the Word was a god" rather than "And the Word was God" because Witnesses deny the divinity of Jesus.
- In Colossians 1:15-20, the word "other" is inserted into the text four times because Witnesses believe that Jesus was created. The word does not appear in the Greek manuscripts.

Now, unless there is an authority outside of the Bible to declare such translations unreliable and dangerous, by what authority could someone call them unsuited for use in teaching doctrine?

Protestants might respond that this issue can be settled on the basis of biblical scholarship, but Jehovah's Witnesses also cite biblical scholarship in support of their translation. The issue then devolves into a game of pitting scholars against scholars, none of whom has any objective authority over any other. The only way to resolve the dilemma is to appeal to something outside the Bible (i.e., beyond the scholars) to see which translation is faithful to what Christians have always believed. But doing this establishes the Catholic position, because it demonstrates that the Bible is always meant to be understood in its proper context: together with Sacred Tradition and the Church's Magisterium.

Protestantism has divorced itself from the Magisterium, and it has no central authority that speaks on behalf of Christ. Hence, it cannot issue an official, divinely safeguarded ruling against faulty or heretical Bible translations. The faithful who are not sufficiently educated to know what to look out for when choosing a Bible version risk being theologically misled and seduced into believing "another" gospel (Gal. 1:6-9).

At best, Protestants can tell us to rely on their Bible scholars, but how should we respond, then, when Jehovah's Witnesses ask, "Why should we trust your scholars rather than ours?" The only acceptable answer to this question is, "Because our scholars translate in a way that harmonizes with the deposit of faith and with what the Church has always believed and taught." But this is the Catholic position, not the Protestant position.

BIBLE-BURNING

It is relevant here to mention and dispel a myth that seems to find new life in every age: that the Catholic Church burned Bibles because it was trying to prevent the faithful from having the scriptures.

Did the Church burn Bibles? Yes . . . but only the translations that were misleading, faulty, heretical, and inconsistent with the Church's living memory—in other words, the ones that advanced their own distorted theological agendas. This is one way that the Church kept the faithful from being seduced by a distortion of the scriptures, which would ultimately lead people into theological darkness.

Protestants may point out that Catholics are in the same situation: we, too, cannot prevent bad translations from being published. This is quite true. However, the critical difference is that Catholics have an infallible guide that speaks for all Christians on behalf of Christ and can warn the faithful about such distortions of God's word *with binding authority*. The warning would not be merely the expressed opinion of some Bible scholars—remember, the Jehovah's Witnesses can also produce scholarly opinions—but is instead the official declaration of a teaching authority guaranteed by Christ to have his protection and the guidance of the Holy Spirit. Protestants, by contrast, are essentially left to a game of "trump the scholar" to resolve such difficulties. The problem with this approach is that they have replaced a divinely mandated, divinely guided teaching authority with one that is merely human in origin and proceeds from a particular denominational affiliation.

Protestants may also say we can "compare Scripture with Scripture" to resolve this kind of problem because all Scripture has the same divine author, and we would expect Scripture to harmonize with Scripture. This is true enough. But if you were to approach the NWT this way, under the guidance of the Watch Tower Society that produced the NWT, you would end up with these beliefs:

- Jesus is not God, but a highly exalted creature, the first of Jehovah God's creations.
- Jesus and Michael the archangel are the same person.
- Jesus came to earth primarily to vindicate Jehovah's good name, which had been called into question by Satan.
- Jesus died on a "torture stake," not a cross.
- Jesus' death was not a substitute ransom to pay for humanity's sins, but a corresponding ransom to precisely counteract what Adam had lost in the Garden of Eden.

Of course, this belief system bears no resemblance to what the Christian faith actually is.

Questions to Ask:

1. On what basis do you tell a Jehovah's Witness that the New World Translation is a bad and biased translation, considering that Jehovah's Witnesses provide scholarly support for their translation?

2. Is appealing to the early Church Fathers and Church councils to show that one translation is better than another, or that one is more in line with historical Christianity than another, more of a Protestant approach or a Catholic approach?

3. If a Bible translation distorts orthodox Christian doctrines, and thus exposes people to false doctrines, what should be done with it?

REASON 21

SOLA SCRIPTURA PRODUCES DIVISION AND DISUNITY

If the doctrine of *sola scriptura* were true, then we would reasonably expect Protestants to be in substantial agreement on doctrine, as the Bible cannot teach contradictory beliefs. And yet the reality is that there are literally thousands of Protestant sects and denominations, each of which claims to have the Bible as its only guide, each of which claims to be preaching the truth, yet each of which teaches something different from the others.

By some estimates, there are 25,000 different Protestant denominations, sects, and groups. Some estimates are as high as 35,000. The exact number doesn't much matter, and a Protestant may insist that there are, for instance, only six major branches within Protestantism, not thousands or tens of thousands. But even six is five too many, because that is five more than the number of churches Jesus founded.

Championing the individual's right to interpret the Bible for himself can only foster division, not unity. When Protestant groups differ on doctrine and cannot reach an accord, they create another version of the Protestant faith. Even the lead Protestant rebels—Luther, Zwingli, and Calvin—couldn't agree on doctrine, which is what led Zwingli and Calvin to depart from Luther and establish their own belief systems. In the process, they set a clear example for others to follow.

Even if we acknowledge the existence of just six major "branches" within Protestantism—Lutheran, Calvinist, Baptist, Methodist, Presbyterian, and Anglican—each of these branches is subdivided into countless variations. Each independent congregation may in general terms call itself, say, Lutheran or Baptist, but what additional changes or additions in doctrine from the original system does it espouse? And what about non-denominational churches? By definition, they are different from the six major Protestant divisions. How many of *those* are there?

Whether it's six denominations or 60,000, all teaching contradictory doctrines, the fact remains: this reality bears no resemblance to the unity for which Christ prayed in John 17.

Protestants have an oft-quoted phrase: "In essentials unity, in non-essentials liberty, in all things charity."[74] But they don't have unity even in Christian doctrinal essentials like the Eucharist, salvation, and justification. Or we might be told, "The main things are the plain things, and the plain things are the main things."[75] But beneath this catchy syntax lies the reality that Protestants *don't agree* on the main things, and *not* everything in Scripture is plain (recall 2 Pet. 3:16).

For instance, most Protestant groups teach that Jesus Christ is only *symbolically* present in the Eucharist, but some, such as Episcopalians and Lutherans, believe that he is literally present, at least to some extent or in some way. Some maintain that once you are "saved," you cannot lose your salvation, whereas others believe that it is possible for a Christian to sin gravely and cease being "saved." Some teach that you can lose your salvation but then regain it. And some teach that justification involves the Christian being *declared* righteous (a forensic or judicial act), whereas others teach that the Christian should grow in holiness and actually *become* righteous through grace.

Now let's drill the point home with arguably the most important of the above doctrines: the real presence of Jesus Christ in the Eucharist. If "the plain things are the main things," why do most Protestants deny the Real Presence? How can this be, in light of Jesus' *exceedingly plain* words in the Bread of Life Discourse in John 6:22-59? Here Jesus says some explicit things:

> Truly, truly, I say to you, unless you eat the flesh of the Son of man and drink his blood, you have no life in you; he who eats my flesh and drinks my blood has eternal life, and I will raise him up at the last day. For my flesh is food indeed, and my blood is drink indeed. He who eats my flesh and drinks my blood abides in me, and I in him (vv. 53-56).

Most Protestants distort the clear meaning of this passage. For example, James White says,

> *A literal interpretation is one that takes the intentions of the author seriously and, hence, will allow for different ways of speaking*. For example, when Jesus utilizes symbolic language in John 6, he lays out his meaning first by defining his terms, saying that those who hunger and thirst are coming and believing in him (v. 35). He defines the categories of hungering and thirsting as non-physical spiritual realities. Therefore, when he

> later speaks of eating his flesh and drinking his blood (vv. 53-58), he has already categorized such language; accordingly, the *literal* reading of his words is to read them *spiritually* (as v. 36 indicates) rather than *physically* (which would violate the definitions he himself had established).[76]

Let's examine this passage (John 6:22-59) to see if what White claims is accurate.[77] We will look at the verses that mention bread and eating, and we will see that White's claim that Jesus categorizes his own words as spiritual—that is, metaphorical—is wrong.

In fact, Jesus categorizes his words as literal multiple times:

Verse 26: Jesus challenges the crowds' motivation for seeking him out. They are merely interested in another free meal. The "loaves" are literal bread.

Verse 27: Jesus invites them to think not just on an earthly level, but on a heavenly or spiritual level. "Food" here is literal food, because its antecedent is "loaves" in the preceding verse.

Verse 31: The "manna" and "bread" are literal food, not symbols.

Verse 32: Jesus reminds his audience that the manna was provided by the Father, not Moses. It's still literal food.

Verse 33: Just as the desert manna was the "bread of God," Jesus is showing how that manna prefigured him as the "bread of God" in the Eucharist. He is beginning to move his audience members from an earthly reality to a heavenly reality.

Verse 34: In typical Johannine fashion, Jesus' audience misunderstands him. Jesus will correct and elevate their thinking shortly, but the "bread" is still literal food.

Verse 35: Jesus uses "hunger" and "thirst" in a spiritual sense—not a metaphorical sense—but this is consistent with his desire to get his audience to understand the higher spiritual reality of the Real Presence. There is a definite shift in verse 51 to that doctrine.

White claims that Jesus is "categorizing" his language in this verse, but from the beginning of the Bread of Life Discourse until now, Jesus has consistently been referring to "bread" and "manna" in a literal way. He will continue to do so in the verses that follow.

Jesus' use of a spiritual meaning in this verse is his way of moving his audience from a mere earthly understanding of his words to a heavenly understanding. It is *not* a move from a literal understanding to a metaphorical one. Jesus' words "I am the bread of life" make perfect sense when properly understood in reference to the Eucharist and in the context of mentioning the desert manna—which the entire discourse makes clear. The bread is *still* literal. Up through and including this verse, literal food has been mentioned in seven out of seven verses.

White is correct that Jesus has categorized his language: he is speaking literally, and even though Jesus repeats this reality multiple times to emphasize it and make it perfectly clear, White seems to miss the point. *This* is why Jesus set up his Church's Magisterium.

Verse 41: The Jews "murmur" because they understand Jesus' words about "the bread that came down from heaven" literally.

Verse 48: We have to understand these words in light of the verses that precede them (repeated literal bread) and those that immediately follow. Jesus calls himself "the bread of life," and then immediately refers back to *literal* manna in the next verse because he is going to emphasize a literal bread—his body—that is far more important than the desert bread.

Verse 49: The "manna" is still literal food.

Verse 50: Both "bread" and "eat" are literal. For Jesus to immediately jump to metaphorical language after having established the literal dimension of the manna and after having emphasized literal bread in multiple verses is untenable.

Verse 51: The "bread" here is identified by Jesus as being his "flesh." This is not the language of metaphor, and we cannot dismiss the parallels Jesus is making to the desert manna, a bread that came from heaven and that gave literal (earthly) life.

Verse 52: The Jews do *not* understand Jesus metaphorically, as White claims. They understand him on a literal level.

Verse 53: Not only does Jesus *not* correct their literal understanding of his words, but he *emphasizes* that understanding, and he underscores the importance of his teaching by introducing it with a double "amen," a literary device used for emphasis. There is no language or context that indicates the use of metaphor here.

Verse 54: John highlights Jesus' shift to the Real Presence—but it's still a move from literal to literal—by using a different Greek word for "eat"—namely, one that has the more graphic meaning of "munch" or "gnaw," apparently as his way of emphasizing the reality of Jesus' presence in the Eucharist.[78] This word is *not* the language of metaphor, and for Jesus to shift to a more graphic verb to indicate an alleged metaphorical meaning would make no sense.

Verse 55: Jesus cannot be any clearer. His flesh is *true* food, and his blood is *true* drink. This yet again is the language of not metaphor, but emphatic reality. Jesus would be an exceedingly bad teacher if, after all his stress on literal eating and literal food in this discourse, he uses even more emphatic language—but only to make a sudden and dramatic shift to establish a metaphorical point instead. Not only this, but he would also contradict what comes next, in verses 60-69, where we see the following:

1) Jesus' own disciples understand him literally (v. 60),
2) Jesus does *not* correct them for understanding his words literally (v. 61),
3) Jesus allows his own followers to leave him instead of compromising the doctrine of the Real Presence (v. 66), and
4) Jesus turns to his apostles, ready to allow *them* to leave also before he would compromise his teaching on the Real Presence (v. 67).

LITERALLY—NO, REALLY

There are actually three times in this narrative when Jesus does not correct his listeners, because there was no need to: (1) when he identifies himself as the "bread of life" (compare verse 35 with verses

41-43); (2) when he says he will give his flesh to eat (compare verse 51 with verses 52-53); and (3) when he allows some of his listeners to walk away rather than correct their proper understanding of his words (compare verse 60 with verse 66).

If all of this is the language of metaphor, as Protestants insist, then Jesus just delivered one of the most misleading and confusing discourses ever recorded. It is highly more likely that White and all who insist on a metaphorical interpretation are grossly mistaken and are basing their interpretation of this discourse on polemic, denominational affiliation, and denial—not on sound biblical exegesis, and certainty not in accord with the Church's unchanging teaching on the subject.

The truth of the Real Presence is so important that Jesus will allow *nothing* to compromise it. This much is evident from even a surface reading of John 6, yet most branches of Protestantism distort something so "plain" and "main" as the doctrine of the Real Presence.

Getting back to our main point, Jesus never intended for his followers to be as fragmented and disunited as Protestantism has been since its inception. Even the original Protestant leaders—Martin Luther, John Calvin, and Ulrich Zwingli—did not agree on doctrine, and they went so far as to label each other's teachings heretical.

In fact, quite a controversy erupted over the heart of the Christian faith—namely, the real presence of Christ in the Eucharist. Luther affirmed it, more or less, but Calvin and Zwingli vehemently denied it. As the Catholic Church teaches, the Eucharist is the source and summit of unity in the Body of Christ (CCC 1324-1326). Faith in Christ and what he taught is meant to unite believers, not divide them, as Paul says:

> I appeal to you, brethren, by the name of our Lord Jesus Christ, that all of you agree and that there be no dissensions among you, but that you be united in the same mind and the same judgment. For it has been reported to me by Chloe's people that there is quarreling among you, my brethren. What I mean is that each one of you says, "I belong to Paul," or "I belong to Apollos," or "I belong to Cephas," or "I belong to Christ." Is Christ divided? Was Paul crucified for you? Or were you baptized in the name of Paul? (1 Cor. 1:10–13).

If Paul were writing a letter to the Protestant leaders of the sixteenth century, he may have written something like this:

> I appeal to you, brothers, in the name of our Lord Jesus Christ, that all of you stay joined to Christ's Church, and that there be no divisions among you, but that you be united in the same doctrine and in the same liturgical practice. For it has been reported to me about you, my brothers, by the faithful, that there are rivalries and schisms among you. I mean that each of you is saying, "I belong to Luther," or "I belong to Calvin," or "I belong to Zwingli." Is Christ divided? Is Luther the rock upon which Jesus built his Church? Were you baptized in the name of Calvin?

On the contrary, Jesus prayed that his followers "that they may all be one; even as thou, Father, art in me, and I in thee, that they also may be in us" (John 17:21). And Paul exhorts Christians to doctrinal unity with the words, "one body and one Spirit . . . one Lord, one faith, one baptism" (Eph. 4:4–5).

The existence of thousands of Protestant denominations and sects, all of which claim to have the "true gospel," flies in the face of the unity of which Paul spoke. They can't claim unity even on the essentials.

Consider what one modern Protestant minister has to say about the theological chaos that developed after Luther's death. Bear in mind that this description is for what happened just among Lutherans, not long after Luther died. How much more convoluted, then, does the Protestant doctrinal scene become once hundreds—even thousands—of sects within Protestantism develop over time and as more and more conflicting voices add to the cacophony of teachings?

> After Luther's death, there was no lack of doctrinal controversy among the Lutherans.
>
> There was the Adiaphoristic Controversy (whether some abolished ceremonies neither commanded nor forbidden in Scripture must be reestablished for the sake of peace), the Majoristic Controversy (whether good works are necessary for salvation), and the Synergistic Controversy (whether man contributes anything to his conversion).
>
> There was also the Flacian Controversy (whether original sin is the very essence of man's nature or a very deep corruption of it) and the Osiandrian and Stancarian Controversies (whether our righteousness comes from God's declaration that our sins are forgiven for Christ's sake or if it is infused by Christ dwelling in us, causing us to be righteous and do righteous things). The Antinomian Controversy (whether Christians need the preaching of God's Law and whether there is a Third Use of the Law), the

> Crypto-Calvinistic Controversy (whether Christ's body and blood are received orally under the bread and wine by all who partake or not), and the controversy over Christ's descent into hell all were fought within Lutheranism as well.
>
> In addition to these major controversies, there was trouble brewing over the teaching of predestination and what we can know about it according to the scriptures and what we must leave to the hidden counsel of God in his divine wisdom.[79]

All of these controversies have their origins in *the private interpretation of Scripture.* Isn't it odd that despite Protestant claims that the Bible is the sole, final authority, which is sufficiently clear on the "plain things," there is such a lack of unanimity on these doctrines, even within a single denomination immediately after the death of its founder?

Protestant Objection: But Catholics are in the same situation. You also have your divisions and splinter groups. Catholicism is also fragmented.

Catholic Response: You must first explain what you mean by "fragmented." Sure, there are differences in liturgical rites and practices, for instance, but these things are differences in style, custom, or culture, not necessarily in doctrine.

We agree that there are splinter groups within Catholicism. However, the significant difference is that the Catholic Church can rightly say that such groups broke away from unity with the Church and have no mission that stems from a legitimate source. No Protestant group can validly make this claim.

Given the doctrine of *sola scriptura*, whenever a new Protestant sect arises, the existing groups *should* say, "It's great that you have established yourselves, and we completely support whatever beliefs you derive from the scriptures." But I suspect they might be thinking about the new sects the same way Catholics think about Protestants: "We don't quite agree with you guys because you are misinterpreting the scriptures."

Beyond doctrinal division—we might even say chaos—there were also serious reverberations in society and daily life that were the direct result of Martin Luther's teachings:

> Heresy produces violence, which is why it was considered both an ecclesiastical and secular crime in the sixteenth century. As with earlier heresies, violence followed the religious discussions resulting from the Reformation so that "what began as a sort of spiritual family quarrel and continued as a spiritual civil war was soon accompanied by an actual civil war in arms." Europe was engulfed in violence for a century as a result of the Reformation, and the modern world continues to suffer from the teachings that took root in the minds of men during the sixteenth century.[80]

If we take to heart an important standard that Jesus identified, we see that "no good tree bears bad fruit, nor again does a bad tree bear good fruit; for each tree is known by its own fruit" (Luke 6:43-44). But if the direct result of the Reformation was the creation of thousands of separate and conflicting groups, this fact speaks volumes, on a spiritual level, about its origin. Had Luther actually been a reformer, and if he had been used by God to "set things right," then there would not have been such negative and disruptive consequences. On the basis of Jesus' own standard, it is clear that the *sola scriptura* tree is not producing good fruit.

Questions to Ask:

1. How can the doctrinal disagreement that exists among Protestant sects line up with the unity for which Jesus prayed?

2. How many churches did Jesus establish?

3. What marks (identifying characteristics) do the thousands of Protestant groups have that show them to be the one Church established by Jesus?

4. If a given Christian is wrong about such a "plain thing" as Jesus' words in the Bread of Life Discourse, then what other things might he be wrong about?

5. Why didn't the original Protestant leaders agree on their understanding of the Eucharist, and why did they label one another's teachings heretical?

6. According to 1 Corinthians 11:2, Ephesians 5:25-27, and Revelation 19:7, how many brides does Christ have? And so how can Protestantism, with its many competing sects, be the one bride of Christ?

REASON 22

SOLA SCRIPTURA DOES NOT ALLOW FOR A FINAL, DEFINITIVE SCRIPTURE INTERPRETATION

The doctrine of *sola scriptura* claims the Bible as the only rule of faith. Individual believers, the doctrine goes, can arrive at a true interpretation of a Scripture passage simply by comparing it with what the rest of the Bible teaches. In practice, though, this approach creates more problems than it solves, and it ultimately prevents Protestants from knowing with any degree of assurance how any passage from the Bible ought to be interpreted.

In practice, Protestants approach the Bible from a subjective viewpoint (personal interpretation) rather than objective truth (receiving the deposit of faith), or from the bottom (individual) up rather than from the top (hierarchy) down. The result is multiple contradictory interpretations.

Let's take one of the core Protestant beliefs to illustrate: justification by faith alone. We might think that on a central doctrine for Protestants, there would be unanimity as to what it means and how it applies to the life of a believer based on what the New Testament says on the issue. But this is not actually the case. Protestants routinely stand on opposite sides of crucial doctrines, as Jimmy Akin notes. Here it is worth quoting him at length:

> Although the phrase "justification by faith alone" is universal in Protestant churches, how it is understood—and the "works" it is meant to exclude—varies from one group to another. . . .
>
> At one end of the spectrum is a position found in some parts of Evangelicalism known as *free grace theology*. It holds that you have saving faith as long as you intellectually assent to certain theological truths, though there is debate on which ones. Some free grace advocates hold that all you need to believe is that Jesus Christ will save you. Others argue that you must include additional beliefs. . . .
>
> The free grace view is sometimes disparaged as "easy believism" by its critics. Free grace theologians, in turn, accuse their critics of "legalism."

More specifically,

> the New Testament also contains passages linking baptism to salvation (Acts 2:38, 22:16; Rom. 6:3–4; 1 Pet. 3:21), which has prompted discussion of how this may be squared with *sola fide*. Lutherans understand the formula in a way that does not exclude baptism as a means of justification, as do some Anglicans, Presbyterians (in the case of elect infants), and members of the Church of Christ movement. Yet many other

> Protestants see the idea of baptism as a means of salvation as a violation of the "faith alone" formula.
>
> If we are saved through faith, what happens if a person loses faith? According to some Protestant authors, it does not matter. Even a single moment of saving faith will result in a person being saved for all time. . . . Others hold that it is not possible for a person to lose saving faith. . . . Still others hold that a loss of faith—and *only* a loss of faith—will cause one to lose salvation. . . .
>
> But if salvation can be lost, can it be regained? Some Lutherans have held that salvation cannot be regained. However, most Protestants who believe that salvation can be lost also hold that it is possible to reacquire it by once again repenting and having saving faith.[81]

Without an infallible authority to tell Protestants which one of their respective interpretations is correct (if any), there is no way for them to know if they possess truth or error. Protestants are ultimately left to individual interpretations based on personal opinion. Study and research don't change that fact. Each Protestant thus becomes his own final authority—his own pope. Martin Luther said as much:

> In these matters of faith, to be sure, each Christian is for himself pope and church.[82]
>
> Besides that, we are all priests [by virtue of baptism] as I have said, and have all one faith, one gospel, one sacrament; how then should we not have the power of discerning and judging what is right or wrong in matters of faith? . . . We should boldly judge what they

> [popes] do and what they leave undone by our own believing understanding of the scriptures.[83]

Luther not only railed with pathological hatred against the pope, but also effectively made himself a pope by setting himself up as the sole arbiter of the meaning of Scripture. He got angry and belligerent (and that is putting it mildly) when others didn't agree with him. It would seem that Luther intended the *sola scriptura* rule of private interpretation to apply only to him.

Since Protestants cannot agree on their interpretations, every Protestant group necessarily arrives at its own. But if there are many interpretations of Scripture, by definition, there is no ultimate interpretation. And if there is no ultimate interpretation, then people cannot know if their interpretations are objectively true—that is, in harmony with what the biblical authors intended to convey and what the apostles taught.

This is not to deny that Scripture can have different levels of meaning in terms of its application in the life of a believer. But two opposing interpretations of a given passage cannot both be true.

Take the doctrine of the Real Presence as an example. If one person says that, once they are consecrated, the bread and wine at Mass actually become the body and blood of Jesus Christ, and another person says they do not, both views cannot be correct. In fact, one view *has* to be wrong because there is no third option. Or if one person says baptism is necessary for salvation and another says it is an important symbol but not a requirement to be saved, it is impossible for both views to be correct.

A good comparison here is the moral law. If each person relies on his own judgment to determine right from wrong, we end up with nothing more than moral relativism, and everyone asserts his own set of standards. (Isn't this our lived reality in the twenty-first century?) However, God has clearly defined moral absolutes for us in Scripture—in addition to those we can know by reason from the natural law—so we can assess any given behavior or thought and determine its moral value, good or bad. This assessment would be impossible without moral absolutes, which serve as fixed points from which we measure how near or far things are from them. In a similar way, there are scriptural "absolutes"—that is, certain interpretations that do not allow for contradictory ones.

Each Protestant group necessarily maintains that its interpretations are the correct ones—in practice, if not formally. If this were not so, its adherents would be hard-pressed not to change affiliations, or make new ones. However, if any group claims that its interpretations are correct, it has effectively made them superior to those of the other groups and, in the process, set itself up as a final authority or arbiter of scriptural truth. All of this is done under the guise of *sola scriptura*, and it means that *sola scriptura* becomes the basis for multiple doctrinal positions, even contradictory ones.

SCRIPTURE, FORMALLY DEFINED

Romans 5:12 refers to original sin. John 3:5 shows the necessity of the sacrament of baptism. James 5:14-15 refers to the sacrament of anointing of the sick. John 20:22-23 refers to the sacrament of reconciliation. The words of institution in the synoptic Gospels ("this is my body," "this is my blood") teach the real presence of Christ in the Eucharist.

On the other hand, in the unlikely event of one group admitting that its interpretations are no more trustworthy than those of other groups, we are back to the original dilemma of never knowing which interpretation is accurate and thus never having the definitive truth. It would also mean that it doesn't matter what your denominational affiliation is. But the Lord said, "I am the way, and the truth, and the life" (John 14:6). His truth is a single body of teachings he gave to the apostles with the command to spread them to "all nations" (Matt. 28:19-20).

The insurmountable predicament here is that every Protestant group treats its interpretations as correct. (Have you ever known a group to assert, "This is what we believe, but we certainly could be wrong!"?) We are thus left with thousands of different groups, each one claiming to impart "what the Bible teaches," yet none of which can provide an objective validation of or reason for its claim. The result is either the acceptance and spread of heterodoxy or an inability to arrive at a decisive interpretation of any Scripture passage. Neither one is okay.

In this regard, Protestant groups truly are following their founder's example. From the beginning, Luther seemed confused about a whole range of theological issues, unable to settle them definitively by using "only Scripture":

> Ever vacillating, ambiguous, contradictory, he was utterly incapable of formulating a clear, well-defined, unhesitating system of belief to replace that of the old divinely established Church.
>
> It was a special characteristic of him, as every student of his life knows, to deny one day what he professed the day before. At one moment he would declare the Church infallible, and the next he would say it is fallible. He urged that all should submit to the councils of the Church, and then that they must not. He maintained that the civil government had power over the ministers of religion, and then denied

it. He admitted that there was a hell, and afterward questioned its existence. He taught that the sacraments conferred grace and advocated the contrary. He claimed that there were seven sacraments, and then reduced them to two, increased them to three, and finally to five. He maintained each of the sacraments and denied five of them. In baptism, he both admitted and denied that grace was conferred, and taught that original sin was effaced and that it was not. He maintained that there was a purgatory and that we should pray for the dead, and then denied it.[84]

Protestant Objection: Catholics have the same problem, though. The Church has formally defined the meaning of only a small number of Bible passages, so it seems as though Catholics are free to read the Bible with their own understanding and interpretations just as Protestants.

Catholic Response: It is true that the Church has defined only a small number of Bible passages. In each case, however, the passage deals directly with a doctrine (as opposed to an exhortation, a good example, and the like). Apart from formally defined verses, the Church also sets forth biblical meanings and doctrinal teachings in its ordinary and universal Magisterium—that is, what the Church has consistently taught everywhere.

Finally, although Catholics are free to interpret the Bible on their own, they are not at liberty to adhere to an interpretation that contradicts either the ordinary Magisterium or those passages that have been formally defined. Catholics, therefore, have both the liberty to interpret the Bible and clear guidance on its meaning. The Church also sets forth guidelines on how to read and approach the scriptures in documents like *The Interpretation of the Bible in the Church*, which was presented by the Pontifical Biblical Commission to Pope John Paul II in 1993 and published in 1994.

In a best-case scenario, Protestants, by contrast, can assert only that someone's interpretation of a Bible passage may differ from theirs. They cannot make a definitive or binding ruling on that interpretation because there is no central authority in Protestantism to stand behind it. Furthermore, one Protestant cannot legitimately tell another that his interpretation of a Bible passage is wrong, because *sola scriptura* is predicated on the right to private interpretation.

Questions to Ask:

1. How do Protestants know if their interpretation of any given Bible passage is accurate? How can they be sure they are not twisting or distorting the scriptures (2 Pet. 3:16)?

2. Can opposite interpretations of the same Bible passage both be true? If two Protestant groups teach opposite interpretations of a Bible passage, doesn't one group have to be wrong?

3. Is it okay to switch denominations to find one that agrees with your particular interpretation of Scripture? If so, doesn't this suggest that interpretations are relative rather than objectively true?

4. If Luther was guided by the Holy Spirit, then why do his doctrinal positions change or contradict one another? Is such vacillation a sign of the Spirit's presence or guidance?

5. Can you cite any New Testament passages where Jesus sends out his disciples to preach and tells them to allow people to interpret Scripture however they want?

REASON 23

PROTESTANT BIBLICAL AIDS MILITATE AGAINST *SOLA SCRIPTURA*

There is no shortage of available resources for Protestants who want to read the Bible and better understand its contents. In light of the Protestant claim that the Bible is self-interpreting, you would think these resources would be superfluous. After all, doesn't the Holy Spirit guide our understanding of the Bible? And though the Bible may be hard to understand in some places, isn't it sufficiently clear in other places? Haven't we already seen above that "the main things are the plain things, and the plain things are the main things"?

The existence of all these biblical aids presents yet another problem. Either the Bible is not sufficiently clear, not easy to understand, and not "plain" on the main things—as evidenced by the existence of such aids—or the authors and publishers of these aids are effectively serving as a magisterium for Protestants by guiding their understanding of its contents—which, ironically, is precisely the arrangement that Luther rejected.

Protestant Objection: Your objection is absurd. Of *course* we should seek help from such aids so we can better understand what the Bible means. After all, it was written long ago, and anyone who is serious about understanding it can gain much through these resources.

Catholic Response: We agree that such resources are helpful, but that is not the issue here. If Christians are at liberty to interpret the Bible however they may, and if the Bible is sufficiently clear, as Protestants also allege, then why not leave it at that? The Westminster Confession of Faith states,

> Those things which are necessary to be known, believed, and observed, for salvation, are so clearly propounded and opened in some place of Scripture or other, that not only the learned, but the unlearned, in a due use of the ordinary means, may attain unto a sufficient understanding of them.[85]

Your position is an implied admission that external guidance of some kind or another is an intrinsic component of the Christian faith. The difference between Protestants and Catholics is that although Protestants acknowledge the need for such guidance and help, they turn to someone other than the people whom Jesus himself set in place to function in that capacity.

It would also seem that Protestants don't agree on the extent of the Bible's perspicuity—that is, its self-revealing character. The issue is further compounded by the fact that they don't agree on what items constitute "those things . . . necessary . . . for salvation."

The use of such resources shows that Protestants need, or at least want, additional help, which seems to belie the claims made by them about the Bible's perspicuity. It is also a recognition of the truth of Peter's statement in 2 Peter 3:16 that the Bible is *not* always clear. It is furthermore an indication that Christians will always need guidance in correctly understanding the scriptures—as even Protestants attest in multiple places—which is precisely why Jesus constituted his Church with a teaching Magisterium that is the only authority formally and officially sanctioned by him to provide such guidance. This is precisely the authority that Luther rejected—but which seems to have come alive again in the form of modern biblical resources. Consider a few examples from the Bible that imply a dim view of the Protestant idea of biblical perspicuity:

2 Chronicles 17:7-9: It is striking that King Jehoshaphat sends his official representatives (princes) and those instructed in the law (Levites and priests) to visit the cities of Judah for the explicit purpose of teaching the law to Judah's inhabitants. If they traveled with "the book of the law of the LORD," and if the law were sufficiently clear—remember, the Mosaic Law is the heart of the Jewish faith—then why didn't these three groups of men simply read the law to the people? Why was it necessary, even commanded, to teach it?

This passage beautifully prefigures Christ's Church, because in the New Testament, the true king (Jesus) sends out his official representatives (the apostles) with a royal mandate (divine commission) to authoritatively teach the Faith to "all cities" ("all nations," Matt. 28:19). *Never* is anyone told simply to go out and read the scriptures to people and allow them to come to whatever interpretations they may.

Matthew 13:18-23: The Parable of the Sower and the Seed is Jesus' metaphor for "the word of the kingdom." Now, unless Protestants would dare suggest that *any* of Jesus' parables are unimportant, the reality is that Jesus had to explain the meaning of this parable to his disciples. In other words, he had to interpret it for them. It was not sufficiently clear on its own.

Luke 24:27: This is an especially problematic verse for biblical perspicuity. Jesus had to explain *the central message* of the scriptures to these two disciples. One has to maintain either that the scriptures are not sufficiently clear on a major doctrine or that the messianic passages are not "necessary for salvation." Either option proves fatal to the Protestant idea of biblical perspicuity.

Acts 8:30-31: The Ethiopian eunuch is reading a passage from the prophet Isaiah, and he specifically tells Philip that he doesn't understand it. It happens that the passage he is reading is a prophetic utterance about Jesus' passion and death—the central message of the Christian faith.

This passage—*the* major doctrine—is unclear to the eunuch, so Philip interprets it for him and uses it as a starting point to proclaim the gospel.

Moreover, the Holy Spirit tells Philip to approach the eunuch. If the scriptures were sufficiently clear, why would the Holy Spirit send Philip? Why wouldn't the Holy Spirit just speak to the eunuch's heart and give him the kind of interior illumination of which Protestants speak? This would have been the perfect opportunity for such a thing, but the Holy

Spirit instead sends someone who has an official and legitimate Church mandate to speak and teach in its name. This is the Catholic position.

Questions to Ask:

1. When you read something in a Bible aid that contradicts what you believe, what happens?

2. If you find that interpretations of a Bible passage from two different resources don't agree, what should be done? How can you tell if one is correct—assuming that both of them are not faulty?

3. When Protestants assert that the Bible is sufficiently clear on at least the things necessary for salvation, does that effectively mean that the Holy Spirit included material in the Bible that has no real or direct impact on whether or not a person gets to heaven?

4. Who sits in judgment of what biblical content is "necessary" for salvation?

5. If the average Protestant disregards biblical aids, is his salvation in jeopardy? If not, then what practical use are they? If so, then which sect or group should you consult for such aids, and why?

6. Why do Protestants assert that the Bible is sufficiently clear when the Bible itself says otherwise in 2 Peter 3:16, and strongly implies a lack of clarity in places like Nehemiah 8:8, Matthew 13:18-23, and Luke 24:27? If the Bible is clear, why is interpretation necessary in these instances?

7. If the Bible is sufficiently clear on major doctrines, then why are there disagreements—sometimes heated ones—among Protestants on major doctrines like the Eucharist, baptismal regeneration, and eternal security, to name a few?

REASON 24

MARTIN LUTHER INJURES *SOLA SCRIPTURA*'S CREDIBILITY

This may sound harsh, but a look at Martin Luther's life, works, and behavior makes it difficult to come to any other conclusion.

To start with, Luther was persistently and deeply troubled by doubts and despair about his salvation. By his own admission, he felt powerless in the face of temptation and sin:

> My spirit was completely broken and I was always in a state of melancholy; for, do what I would, my "righteousness" and my "good works" brought me no help or consolation.[86]

It is important to assess the impact of this state of mind on the origin of Luther's *sola scriptura* doctrine. Even a cursory examination will show that the doctrine, far from being of divine origin, can be explained as being born of Luther's desire to free himself from the chronic guilty feelings, despair, and temptations that prevented him from having peace of mind and spirit. As Ockham's Razor suggests, between the simpler explanation and the more complex one, the former is probably correct.

Luther admitted to an obsessive concern with his own sinfulness and his inability to resist temptation, so it seems reasonable to conclude that he suffered from *scrupulosity*, or excessive, baseless anxiety about having committed (usually imagined) sins. A scrupulous person often amplifies the severity of his perceived sinfulness, which leads to a lack of trust in God to forgive him. In the words of the International OCD Foundation:

> **What is Scrupulosity?**
> *Scrupulosity* is a subtype of obsessive compulsive disorder (OCD) involving religious or moral obsessions. Scrupulous individuals are overly concerned that something they thought or did might be a sin or other violation of religious or moral doctrine.
>
> **What are the symptoms of scrupulosity?**
> Common obsessions seen in scrupulosity include excessive concerns about:
>
> - fear of committing blasphemy, or offending/angering God
> - behaving overly morally
> - fear of going to hell or being punished by God
> - doubting what you truly believe or feel
> - fear of death
> - needing to acquire certainty about religious beliefs

Behavioral compulsions may include:

- excessive confession
- repeatedly seeking assurance from religious leaders and loved ones[87]

The following excerpts, which are just a sampling, demonstrate evidence of Luther's scrupulosity:

> At these words [prayers in the Mass] I was totally stupefied and terror-stricken. I thought to myself, "With what tongue shall I address such Majesty, seeing that all men ought to tremble in the presence of even an earthly prince? Who am I, that I should lift up mine eyes or raise my hands to the divine Majesty? The angels surround him. At his nod the earth trembles. And shall I, miserable little pygmy, say 'I want this, I ask for that'? For I am dust and ashes and full of sin and I am speaking to the living, eternal and the true God."[88]
>
> Without confession, he testified, the devil would have devoured him long ago. He confessed frequently, often daily, and for as long as six hours on a single occasion. Every sin in order to be absolved was to be confessed. Therefore the soul must be searched and the memory ransacked and the motives probed. As an aid the penitent ran through the seven deadly sins and the Ten Commandments. Luther would repeat a confession and, to be sure of including everything, would review his entire life until the confessor grew weary and exclaimed, "Man, God is not angry with you. You are angry with God. Don't you know that God commands you to hope?"[89]

> When I was a monk I tried ever so hard to live up to the strict rules of my order. I used to make a list of my sins, and I was always on the way to confession, and whatever penances were enjoined upon me I performed religiously. In spite of it all, my conscience was always in a fever of doubt. The more I sought to help my poor stricken conscience the worse it got. The more I paid attention to the regulations the more I transgressed them.[90]

Scrupulosity "often seems to be based on some psychological dysfunction in the person"[91]—that is, it indicates a mentally unhealthy person.

Other sources also acknowledge that Luther's scrupulosity could well have been a form of OCD. For example,

> even after his ordination in 1507 he was haunted with insecurity over his eternal fate. . . . "Luther described feelings of 'fleshly lust, wrath, hatred, or envy against any brother' which constantly 'vexed' him and would not leave no matter how hard he tried to block them from his mind. He also experienced periods of 'blasphemous' thought that left him confused and disturbed and was tormented by urges to curse God and Jesus." Some would now consider this OCD if being diagnosed today, OCD with obsessive relationship fears and doubts or something some call scrupulosity. . . .
>
> It's also said that when he prayed, Luther was obsessed with images of "the devil's behind" and that he went to confession so often, annoying other priests, which arguably could have been a compulsion to

> "confess" and / or seek reassurance, both of which would be common OCD compulsions.[92]

Luther's obsession with the sacrament of confession is another sign that he suffered from mental illness. The International OCD Foundation notes that behavioral compulsions of OCD could include "excessive trips to confession" and "repeatedly seeking reassurance from religious leaders and loved ones." These apply to Luther. A telling observation of Luther's compulsive behavior, one that also confirms the symptoms of OCD, is as follows:

> Luther took to the confessional like a starving man takes to bread; he couldn't get enough. His confessors soon realized that he was a tortured soul who would launch into impossibly detailed descriptions of even the most minor transgressions, such as spilling his food or arriving late for choir. His confessions could last for hours at a time, and even when he was finished, he would sometimes think of additional sins on his way out and return to confess them.[93]

Luther probably never had a moment of true emotional or psychological peace because his faulty conscience always disturbed him about some matter, real or imagined. God the Father was for him not a loving, heavenly figure, but a source of emotional turmoil:

> This anger of God, which pursued him like his shadow, could only be averted by "his own righteousness," by the "efficacy of servile works." Such an attitude of mind was necessarily followed

> by hopeless discouragement and sullen despondency, creating a condition of soul in which he actually "hated God and was angry at him," blasphemed God, and deplored that he was ever born. This abnormal condition produced a brooding melancholy, physical, mental, and spiritual depression, which later, by a strange process of reasoning, he ascribed to the teaching of the Church concerning good works, while all the time he was living in direct and absolute opposition to its doctrinal teaching and disciplinary code.[94]

Luther wrote of the mental and emotional anguish that consistently troubled him. He referred to these bouts of melancholy and other emotional states as *Anfechtung*, a German word that has no direct parallel or translation in English:

> *Anfechtung* can be used to describe an attack of the devil, a temptation to do evil, or a twisting of lies in the mind. *Anfechtung* can refer to the trials of this world, the affliction of the flesh, or the tribulation of earthly distress and sorrow. Luther's use of the German *Anfechtung* and its Latin counterpart *Tentatio*, is translated by Pieper as "temptation," by Plass as "affliction," and by the English edition of LW [*Luther's Works*] as "tribulation." . . .
>
> This is *Anfechtung*: temptation, tribulation, failure, and sin, compounded by self-examination, condemnation, struggle with faith, fear, attack by Satan, and the terror of deserved judgment.[95]

Luther believed some (most?) of these moments to be satanic attacks—the devil's attempts to get him to stop "reforming" the

Church. In reality, they were almost certainly external projections of an interior struggle. They were hardly *bona fide* demonic attacks, but rather Luther attributing to an outside entity what was nothing more than his own "inner demons."

Hartmann Grisar, a Jesuit expert on Luther, noted the following about Luther's solitude in the Wartburg Castle, where he hid for a time:

> Luther saw the Wartburg filled with devils. This, in part, was the result of the fear of demons which he had imbibed in his youth; while in part it was a consequence of the inquietude caused by his internal doubts and self-reproaches. The voices of self-reproach he imagined to be voices from the satanic empire. . . . Thus convinced of his great struggle against the evil spirits, he discovers, in his own imagination, that they become visible and audible to him. . . .
>
> Luther's visionary experiences cannot be doubted. They were gross imaginings of preternatural annoyances and corroborations, misinterpretations of internal and external experiences which are well established, particularly for the period he spent at the Wartburg. . . . His extremely active imagination rendered him very susceptible to hallucinations and illusions.[96]

Although it is beyond the scope of this book to do an in-depth psychological analysis of Luther, it is relevant to our discussion of *sola scriptura* to note that in addition to his scrupulosity, he had a dysfunctional relationship with his father. Various sources suggest that Luther's parents, the primary authority figures in his life, were physically and emotionally abusive to him. For example,

> Hans Luther, Martin's father, was also religious, but his influence on his son was different. He was a strong, irascible, combative man who was clever and ambitious in business. He was also overbearing and exacting in a way that colored Martin's entire life. [Lyndal] Roper claims that this sometimes bitter relationship played a very important role in his religious and theological development.[97]

> Hans also ruled his son with an iron fist.[98]

> It is hard to be purely reasonable when one confronts an indomitable and implacable father. . . . It is clear that Luther's fear of his father's anger figured significantly in his *Anfechtungen*—his temptations, travails, and tribulations—as he struggled toward an understanding of God, not as a merciless judge but as an all-forgiving redeemer.[99]

Though Luther apparently did not say much about the physical abuse he suffered at the hands of his parents, this particular admission from him is most illuminating:

> My mother once beat me up with a cane for stealing a nut until the blood came. Such strict discipline drove me to the monastery, although she meant well. . . . My father once flogged me so cruelly that I fled away from him, and came to bear a grudge against him. It was a long time until he again won my confidence.[100]

Though Luther initially struggled with much difficulty against his scrupulosity and faulty conscience, and though he blamed himself for his shortcomings and tried to overcome them, it seems that when he could not find peace and success through his own efforts, his only pathway to freedom was to externalize his problems and lay the blame for them on someone else. By constantly railing against the pope as the Antichrist, and by constantly projecting his inner struggles outwardly and labeling the devil as the culprit, Luther could maintain a comfortable psychological stasis.

Because the Church asserted the necessity of believers doing exactly what Luther felt powerless to achieve—that is, perform good works, lest their faith be "dead" (James 2:14-17)—Luther made a drastic decision that "solved" his scrupulosity problem: he rejected the teaching authority of the Church, with the pope at its head, as contrary to the Bible. By claiming *sola scriptura* to be true Christian doctrine, Luther eliminated the authority that repudiated his spiritually dysfunctional teachings. Consequently, it is neither unreasonable nor unthinkable to believe that Luther's doctrine of *sola scriptura* was not a God-given teaching, but simply the outward manifestation of a poor soul's tortured psyche seeking solace.

But it is not as though Luther's challenges are a secret. Some, if not many, Protestants are aware of these shortcomings, yet they remain Protestant and stalwart believers in *sola scriptura*. For example, R.C. Sproul, a well-known Reformed theologian, notes,

> The judgment from the perspective of twentieth-century psychoanalysis has been made that Martin Luther was, in fact, insane. And if you are a Protestant and that verdict is true, this means the roots of

> your own religious persuasion could be traced to that of a madman.[101]

Though Sproul seems to doubt the ability to psychoanalyze Luther 500 years after his death, he does note that Luther was "intemperate," was "clearly neurotic," and "suffered from nervous anxiety." "His phobias were many and legendary," and he was motivated "out of a phobic preoccupation with the wrath of God." Further,

> perhaps the thing that would most indicate his insanity is the apparent commitment to megalomania. How else can you explain a person being willing to defy every authority structure of this world and to stand utterly alone as a young priest against all of the authorities of the church—against the pope, against church counsels, against the finest theologians in the land?

Sproul then offers this explanation for Luther's state of mind:

> The thing that the psychiatrists overlook about this man is this: before Luther ever studied theology, he had already distinguished himself with brilliance as a student of the law. And he took that sharply acute, trained legal mind and applied it to the law of God. Then he would look at the law of God and the fullness of the demands of perfection and analyze himself in light of the holy law of God.
>
> And he couldn't stand the results. He kept evaluating himself, not by comparing himself to other human beings, but by looking at the standard of the

> character of God—the righteousness of God. As he saw himself so awful in comparison to the righteousness of God, after a while he began to hate any idea of the righteousness of God.

Finally, Sproul sets aside Luther's flaws to exalt where they led:

> It's like Luther said to the world, from that day forward, to popes and to counsels, to diets and to kings: "The just shall live by faith; justification by faith alone. 'God is holy and I am not' is the article upon which the church stands or falls, and I negotiate it with no one because it is the gospel."
>
> Is that crazy? Ladies and gentlemen, if that's crazy then I pray that God would send an army of insane people like that into this world so that the gospel may not be eclipsed.

We can respect Sproul's vigor here, but we can't ignore how he skips over an unfortunate truth: brilliant men are not invulnerable to tragic flaws, nor are they beyond profound errors in thinking. And so it is not only advisable, but necessary to analyze Luther's doctrines, including *sola scriptura*, in the context of the mind that generated them. We cannot just gloss over this.

The acknowledgment that Protestantism can be traced back to a "madman" is a hard pill to swallow. It cannot easily be explained away. It is possible, as Sproul does, to turn Luther's madness into a sort of virtue, because it led to a critical theological realization from Luther's perspective. And maybe that could squeak by if *sola scriptura* made practical sense. But it doesn't.

Isaac Newton may have been quirky, but his laws of motion *work*. Martin Luther's quirks, on the other hand, only underline the practical problems with *sola scriptura*.

Questions to Ask:

1. Given how Luther described his mental anguish, compulsiveness, and suffering, is it possible that he formed new doctrines to cope with his personal problems?

2. If *sola scriptura* originated in Luther's unhealthy mental state, is it more or less likely to be a God-given doctrine?

3. When someone is considering a branch of Christianity to follow, should the mental state of the branch's founder factor in the decision?

REASON 25

SOLA SCRIPTURA ORIGINATED IN AND WAS SUSTAINED BY THE SPIRIT OF REBELLION

When the New Testament speaks about evidence of the Holy Spirit at work, it speaks of peace, unity, harmony, and love. For example, in Galatians, Paul tells us how to know that the Holy Spirit is at work: "The fruit of the Spirit is love, joy, peace, patience, kindness, goodness, faithfulness, gentleness, self-control" (5:22-23). By contrast, when disobedience, rebellion, and discord are the order of the day, there is a different spirit at work:

> Now the works of the flesh are plain: immorality, impurity, licentiousness, idolatry, sorcery, enmity, strife, jealousy, anger, selfishness, dissension, party spirit, envy, drunkenness, carousing, and the like. I warn you, as I warned you before, that those who do such things shall not inherit the kingdom of God (vv. 19-21).

Let's look at a few of the prominent biblical examples of rebellious attitudes and their consequences.

Adam and Eve: For disobeying God and eating the forbidden fruit, they were banished from paradise. They lost their communion not only with God, but also with each other and with the rest of creation. Sickness, suffering, and death resulted. (See Gen. 3:19, 23-24; Rom. 8:19-22. See also CCC 402-409.)

Moses: Moses disobeyed God's command to *speak* to a rock to bring forth water in the desert, preferring to strike the rock. As punishment, God did not allow Moses to see the promised land, even though Moses had been leading the Israelites in the desert *for forty years* (see Num. 20:7-13).

Israelites: The Israelites wanted a king to rule them, just like the pagan nations. God took this as rebellion and pointed it out to his people, but he allowed them to exercise their free will and to suffer the consequences (see 1 Sam. 8:1-9). There are many other examples of Israel's rebellion against God, but I need not multiply them here.

Rebellion is such a destructive violation of the order and authority God has established that in the Old Testament, it is classified with divination* (see 1 Sam. 15:23). If you are wondering what the connection is between the two, consider that rebellion is essentially the willingness to be led by another spirit—a spirit that is not of God—which is also what happens when a person practices divination or other forms of occultism.

* Some translations, such as the King James Version, American Standard Version, Douay-Rheims, and Good News Translation, render the Hebrew word *qesem* as "witchcraft."

To willfully disregard, challenge, violate, reject, or hold in contempt legitimate authority was considered an egregious sin in the time of Moses, and according to the same Jewish scriptures Jesus appealed to in his preaching. As for Martin Luther, he flatly and bombastically rejected Church authority. It is not easy to turn the same rebellion that condemned so many people (and peoples!) in the Bible into a virtue in this one case.

A Protestant might respond that Luther was reacting to what he perceived as the corrupt Church leadership of his day. There are multiple problems with his approach:

1) It is impossible to discern an objective divine mandate for Luther's particular form of reaction—certainly not from Church authorities, but also not from God. There was no basis to his authority other than his own claim to it. This is hardly how Christ's Church works.

2) The Catholic Church can demonstrate its unbroken lineage all the way back to Jesus and the apostles, and since Jesus promised to protect and accompany the Church always, it *can't* be an illegitimate authority. For the Church to have become corrupt to the extent that Luther maintained would mean that Jesus was remiss in keeping his promises and allowed his Church—his bride and his mystical body—to fall into error.

3) There are two significant examples in the New Testament where Jesus recognized a sinful person's authority: the seat of Moses (Matt. 23:1-3) and Judas Iscariot (see Mark 3:13-19, where Judas is among "the Twelve" and has authority to preach and drive out demons). Although Jesus condemned sinful behavior in both instances, he acknowledged the positions of those he condemned as nevertheless legitimate.

Jesus taught, "The scribes and the Pharisees sit on Moses' seat; so practice and observe whatever they tell you, but not what they do; for they preach, but do not practice." If Luther had been truly led by God, he would have followed Jesus' example by validating the office but condemning the hypocritical behavior. Instead, he rebelled against the office and persuaded others to follow his lead.

4) Because the Church consists of humans, there will always be corruption. Yes, this is a problem. The Church's leaders *should* live to a higher standard . . . but fomenting rebellion against their offices when they are sinful is not the solution. It only adds to the problem.

5) Luther set himself up as sole arbiter of valid doctrine, unaccountable to anyone. But the Church has never worked this way—no one just sets himself up as the supreme authority. Even the pope is elected!

6) Reform, not rebellion, is the appropriate response to hypocritical Church leadership. True reformers will lead by example and draw others to it. St. Francis of Assisi is a fabulous example of such reform. He didn't leave the Church or incite others to rebel against it; he led a life of incredible holiness and transformed the Church from within.

Interestingly, the second half of 1 Samuel 15:23, which compares rebellion to divination, reads, "And stubbornness [*arrogance* in some translations] is as iniquity and idolatry." Why would these two things be equated? Because with stubbornness, a person refuses to submit to correction and express repentance and instead insists on exalting the self above all other concerns.

In other words, stubbornness can make an idol of the self. We saw Luther exhibit this exact attitude when he was confronted by John Eck, Richard von Greiffenklau, and John Cochlaeus. See also this quotation, attributed to Luther, showing how he defended his doctrine of salvation by faith alone (as he understood it):

> This article shall remain in spite of all the world. It is I, Martin Luther, evangelist, who say it. Let no one therefore attempt to infringe it, neither the emperor of the Romans, nor of the Turks, nor of the Tartars, neither the pope, nor the monks, nor the nuns, nor the kings, nor the princes, nor all the devils in hell. If they attempt it, may the infernal flames be their recompense. What I say here is to be taken for an inspiration of the Holy Ghost.[102]

Unfortunately, the conditions in Europe were ripe for widespread rebellion against the Catholic Church. It is beyond the scope of this book to explore them, but it is enough here to say that Luther was the spark that set things ablaze, and the flames he started were fanned by a spirit of anger, violence, greed, and lawlessness among the people.

When fire is contained, it provides illumination and warmth, but when it rages out of control, it causes destruction and death. Luther's "fire" resulted in the fragmentation of Christianity, a rejection of the authority Jesus established by people who claim to be his followers, a corruption of "the faith which was once for all delivered to the saints," and a wresting of Scripture from the context in which it had always functioned. The "great reformer" left theological and spiritual devastation in his wake.

The words written by St. James long ago apply here. He also used fire imagery.

> Let not many of you become teachers, my brethren, for you know that we who teach shall be judged with greater strictness. For we all make many mistakes, and if anyone makes no mistakes in what he says he is a perfect man, able to bridle the whole body also.
>
> If we put bits into the mouths of horses that they may obey us, we guide their whole bodies. Look at the ships also; though they are so great and are driven by strong winds, they are guided by a very small rudder wherever the will of the pilot directs. So the tongue is a little member and boasts of great things. How great a forest is set ablaze by a small fire!
>
> And the tongue is a fire. The tongue is an unrighteous world among our members, staining the whole body, setting on fire the cycle of nature, and set on fire by hell (James 3:1-6).

The system of civil authority, as corrupt as it may be, is willed by God to restrain humanity's lawlessness (Rom. 13:1-7, 2 Tim. 2:1-2). The system of Church authority, as corrupt as some of its individual leaders may have been, is nonetheless willed by Christ to be the means by which the faithful are assured of doctrinal purity and moral guidance. Remember that Jesus chose Judas Iscariot to be an apostle, knowing full well what Judas would end up doing (John 6:64, 13:11). Even Church leadership will never be free from sin—and sometimes even manifestly gross sin—on this side of heaven.

EVE'S THREE EXCUSES

As Genesis 3:6 shows, Eve thought that the forbidden fruit "was good for food, and that it was a delight to the eyes, and that the tree was desired to make one wise."

At the same time, when people sustain a spirit of rebellion and use their own perceived excuses to justify their actions—all in the name of Christ—it is a deeply problematic approach. It is worth noting that

> all revolutions by nature foster division and violence, and these elements were present in the Reformation from the beginning. The Reformers rebelled against the teaching authority of the Catholic Church as exercised by the Roman pontiff and the bishops united with him. Indeed, one of the hallmarks of Protestant teaching was a rejection of papal authority—the very office Christ established to be a sign and source of unity in the Church.[103]

Which is the more likely scenario: that Jesus gave us the office of the pope for the express purpose of maintaining Church unity and then allowed it to become corrupt beyond recognition, and in the process violated his promise to his Church and left it an abandoned bride, or that a dysfunctional man with a rebellious heart and the power of persuasion started a rebellion, and others—for all kinds of reasons that stem from our fallen human nature—followed suit and justified their actions in the process?

This is something we humans are particularly good at. After all, starting all the way back in the Garden of Eden, Eve justified her rebellion against God in herself *three* ways. Humans have been doing it ever since, which is precisely why we need a divinely established authority to safeguard us against justifying or rationalizing our own sins. Jesus gave us this authority in the pope and the Magisterium.

Questions to Ask:

1. Whenever the spirit of rebellion is mentioned in the Bible, is it approved or condemned?

2. Which of two possibilities should we accept: Jesus allowed his Church to apostatize, or Luther was mistaken?

3. How do reform and rebellion differ, and why does it matter?

4. If Luther could rebel against the authority of Christ's Church, then shouldn't others be allowed to rebel against Luther, too? Where does it stop—and is this what the Church is supposed to look like?

PART II:
THE BOAR IN THE VINEYARD

LUTHER BEHIND THE CURTAIN

In *Exsurge Domine*, the bull in which Pope Leo X formally condemns Martin Luther's heretical teachings, the pope refers to Luther as "the wild boar from the forest" who seeks to destroy the vineyard, "an image of the triumphant Church"[104] entrusted to Peter.

The comparison of Luther to a wild boar is appropriate for two reasons: (1) wild boars are aggressive, short-tempered, and easily provoked, and they will not hesitate to attack humans,[105] and (2) they are "potential carriers of viral, bacterial, and parasitic diseases that can affect livestock, wildlife, and humans."[106] Luther was certainly aggressive and short-tempered, and he didn't hesitate to verbally attack anyone who would stand in his way or demonstrate his errors. Moreover, the new doctrines he spread can reasonably be said to have made many people spiritually ill.

Not surprisingly, *Exsurge Domine* was ill received by Luther. Though the bull was intended as a corrective measure to bring Luther to his senses, he dug in his heels:

> This bull condemns Christ himself. It summons me not to an audience but to a recantation. I am going to act on the assumption that it is spurious, though I think it is genuine. Would that Charles [V, Holy Roman Emperor] were a man and would fight for Christ against these Satans. But I am not afraid. God's will be done. . . .
>
> I am sending you a copy of the bull that you may see the Roman monster. The faith and the Church are at stake. I rejoice to suffer in so noble a cause. I am not worthy of so holy a trial. I feel much freer now that I am certain the pope is Antichrist.[107]

With Leo's "wild boar" imagery in mind, it would be helpful to revisit, in detail, the kind of person Luther was. I am not looking to do an extensive psychological treatment of the man, but I do think it's productive to give the reader a working view of Luther because it sets his doctrines in their proper context: a dark heart gives rise to dark ideas. Even a cursory examination of Luther will show that his teachings are an inevitable extension of his rebellious and caustic character and his emotional instability.

One Lutheran observed, "His personality dare not be discounted in assessing how he came to his formulation of the biblical message."[108] I agree completely. Taking this observation to heart, let's have another look at Luther's personality.

We can allow for Luther's fallen humanity—after all, we all possess it—but we also must acknowledge that his unstable temperament, volatile nature, and chronic venting of seething anger against the things he perceived as problematic were serious character flaws, not the traits of a saintly reformer. Any treatment of what he taught, then, must be understood in light of the man. And if his doctrines are more easily determined and defined by his personality than by a proper understanding of Scripture, then we should account for that fact.

Protestant Objection: The claim that Luther was insane, possessed, or something to that effect has certainly been raised before. Protestants don't find it a convincing reason to reject his teachings. After all, even insane people can speak the truth.

Catholic Response: Granted, insane people can say things that are true, but we would expect this to be in the form of the occasional nugget of truth or isolated insight, not an entire theological system. We would reasonably expect Luther, as an alleged reformer, to lead by setting a virtuous example in his teachings, speech, and behavior.

But didn't Luther write a lot of unobjectionable and even laudable material, too? Perhaps, but only if we begin with the *a priori* notion that Luther's theology was correct. Whatever Luther might have written at any given time that accords with the Church's perennial teaching—for example, proclaiming the perpetual virginity of Mary—can be set aside, because it did not come from him uniquely. But if Luther's *unique* teachings were heretical, then how can they possibly be construed as good?

Faulty theology does not lead people to a saving knowledge of Christ and his Church. Consider Paul's harsh words in the first chapter of his letter to the Galatians, where he not only chastises them for going over to "another gospel," but also twice says that the person who preaches this other gospel should be "accursed" (vv. 8-9). What Paul uses as the standard of comparison for determining this "other" gospel is the apostolic teaching that was passed on via Sacred Tradition. But Luther not only willfully broke with that apostolic teaching, but also vehemently rejected it. His theology must therefore be "another gospel." Based on Paul's own standard, Luther would be accursed—twice.

Then there is the matter of Luther's speech and behavior. At the end of the day, every individual Christian will have to judge for himself the worthiness of Luther's cause, but nobody can be expected to do so with an incomplete picture of the man.

It is easy to find many Protestant sources extolling the "good" about Luther. Here—remembering St. James's admonition that a spring must not pour forth both fresh and foul water (see James 3:8-12)—we will examine the other side of the coin.

1) Luther broke his monastic vows and convinced others—namely, twelve nuns[109]—to do likewise. A Protestant source notes that Luther "married a runaway nun, Katharina von Bora, which scandalized many." Their actions were a monastic version of adultery (they were already "married" to the Church). This is why the scandal was so widespread.

Why did Luther spurn his vows and marry? To spite the devil,[110] to please his father, and to spite the pope.[111] There is nothing of love or growing in holiness or helping a spouse attain heaven. One Lutheran professor noted that Luther married Katharina von Bora as "an act of protest."[112]

2) Upon starting his trip home after the Schmalkald Convention, Luther gave a "parting benediction" from his wagon to his friends. He made the sign of the cross over them and said, "May the Lord fill you with his blessings and with hatred of the pope."[113]

We mentioned St. James's epistle above, on control of the tongue. His admonition is worth quoting here:

> but no human being can tame the tongue—a restless evil, full of deadly poison. With it we bless the Lord and Father, and with it we curse men, who are made in the likeness of God. From the same mouth come blessing and cursing. My brethren this ought not to be so. Does a spring pour forth from the same opening fresh water and brackish? Can a fig tree, my brethren, yield olives, or a grapevine figs? No more can salt water yield fresh (James 3:8-12).

Could a Christian really ask for the Lord's blessing upon his friends and in the same breath wish evil upon the head of the Church? These two wishes are incompatible—or, as James says, a case of fresh water and brackish.

3) Luther was known for abusive and foul language, even to make theological points. This way of speaking and writing was not limited to one segment of Luther's life; rather, it was characteristic of his rebellion against Christ's Church. For example,

> Luther had a stupendous power of will and a strong determination to pursue an action to the end. He was a charismatic speaker, capable of dominating

an audience. He also exhibited violent anger, both verbally and in writing. Verbal abuse of scholarly opponents was a mainstay of the age, but Luther took the practice to a new level: his writings are filled with crude obscenities, and he frequently used expressions of biological functions to illustrate spiritual truths.[114]

He mocked fellow Reformers, especially Swiss reformer Ulrich Zwingli, and used vulgar language in doing so. In fact, the older he became, the more cantankerous he was. In his later years, he said some nasty things about, among others, Jews and popes and theological enemies, with words that are not fit to print.[115]

He fairly wallows in the mire of base bodily functions, especially in his vigorous denunciation of his opponents. He liked to hurl the most vulgar filth into the faces of his enemies, after he had stirred it up with something akin to glee. He was excelled by no one in this respect.... In this characteristic quality, he stands forth as a giant, even in his earlier writings.[116]

R.C. Sproul said the following about Luther:

In the sixteenth century, it was acceptable in theological disputation to discuss matters in a rather acerbic form of polemical debate instead of a genteel, polite form of dialogue. So, if you read the writings of the sixteenth century on both sides of the controversy, it seems as though these people are ruthless in their attacks upon each other. But even in that crowd of ruthless debate, Martin Luther was in a class by himself. He was so intemperate, so bombastic, and so

> rude at times, that people have even suggested that he suffered from a mental problem.[117]

The Bible has a lot to say about the kind of speech believers should use—and *not* use. It is hard to believe that Luther, a self-professed expert in Scripture, never read such passages. Mind you, this is just a sampling of what the Bible has to say on the subject:

> Not what goes into the mouth defiles a man, but what comes out of the mouth, this defiles a man (Matt. 15:11).

> Let no evil talk come out of your mouths, but only such as is good for edifying, as fits the occasion, that it may impart grace to those who hear (Eph. 4:29).

> Therefore be imitators of God, as beloved children. And walk in love, as Christ loved us and gave himself up for us, a fragrant offering and sacrifice to God. But immorality and all impurity or covetousness must not even be named among you, as is fitting among saints. Let there be no filthiness, nor silly talk, nor levity, which are not fitting; but instead let there be thanksgiving (Eph. 5:1-4).

> Let your speech always be gracious, seasoned with salt, so that you know how you ought to answer every one (Col. 4:6).

> So put away all malice and all guile and insincerity and envy and all slander (1 Pet. 2:1).

Despite the repeated, clear, and consistent counsel of the Bible to guard our words and to speak in a way that honors God, Luther excited his base emotions and spewed forth invective as a matter of habit.

Even Protestants admit that this approach was *characteristic* of Luther. Of particular and relevant note is the following observation, made by a Protestant:

> Luther is . . . famous for scatological abuse, excremental abuse. Let me give you just one example; it's hard to believe that this would be put in a theological treatise, but Luther says to one of his opponents (I'm paraphrasing now): "Why don't you just do it in your pants, roll it up into a sausage, put that sausage around your neck, and then gobble it down?"
>
> Can you imagine this in a theological treatise? There it is, and there are a lot like it, especially in his later writings. You just have to read this stuff to believe it; it's impossible to tell you that it's there unless you read it. But that's why I had to give you something just a little bit filthy.[118]

And remember: "There are a lot like it."

How did Luther justify speaking this way? On his own authority. He even appeared to perceive it as a virtue, as one Protestant author notes:

> By his own admission, Luther was an angry man. Anger was his special sin. But when directed against the enemies of God, anger helped him, he said, to write well, to pray, and to preach: "Anger refreshes

> all my blood, sharpens my mind, and drives away temptations."
>
> Luther knew some were offended by his harshness and anger, but he explained, "I was born to war with fanatics and devils. Thus my books are very stormy and bellicose. I must root out the stumps and trunks, hew away the thorns and briar, fill in the puddles. I am the rough woodsman, who must pioneer and hew a path."[119]

In defense of Luther, Protestants sometimes suggest that he wrote this way only later in life, when he was in declining health and thus more prone to be in a foul mood. Such a claim, however, does not square with the facts:

> In his concluding years, Luther issued several ferocious (and for admirers both then and now, embarrassing) treatises against his opponents. . . . It would be tempting to dismiss these writings as aberrations, as "medieval remnants," or as the simple products of old age or ill health. But we cannot do this. These "last testaments" accurately express Luther's views and are integral to his theology. Luther's poor health and old age may have exacerbated his anger, but these attacks are consistent, in content and passion, with his earlier writings.[120]

Protestant Objection: The use of abusive and foul language was more or less characteristic of the debates of Luther's time, so he did nothing out of the ordinary.

Catholic Response: If Luther was no better than other figures of his time—if he stooped down to their level—then shouldn't that be considered evidence against his "reformer" label? After all, a great reformer leads by example.

4) Luther secretly gave his approval to Philip, Landgrave of Hesse, for bigamy, and when it was discovered that he had done so, he declined to take responsibility for his counsel. He further compounded his sin by advocating lying for "the sake of the Church."

> At the age of nineteen, Philip had married Christine of Saxony, the daughter of Duke George of Ernestine Saxony. Though the union produced nine children, the Landgrave expressed his unhappiness in the marriage.
>
> In the succeeding years, he would appeal to theological advisors—most notably Luther and Melanchthon—for permission to marry another on the grounds that his sexual appetite was not being fulfilled by his present wife. In 1539, presumably under the seal of the confessional, both Luther and Melanchthon capitulated to his requests, and a year later Philip married seventeen-year-old Margaret von der Saale.[121]

It is beyond the scope of this book to discuss what the Bible says about polygamy. Let us instead focus on Luther's comment when it was discovered that he gave his approval to Philip and then wanted to conceal this fact once it became public knowledge. According to Hartmann Grisar, the Jesuit expert on Luther, Luther's response to his secret being divulged was as follows:

> What harm could it do if a man told a good, lusty lie in a worthy cause and for the sake of the Christian Church?[122]

Luther elsewhere said,

> To lie in case of necessity, or for convenience, or in excuse, would not offend God, who was ready to take such lies on himself.[123]

When it comes to "good" and "lusty" lies as a "worthy cause" "for the Church," it is worth checking what Scripture has to say about such matters. According to Jesus, lies originate *in Satan* (John 8:44). It is inconceivable that Luther could think that something satanic could serve the Church or be unoffensive to God. Nor is it a good look for a Christian reformer to presume the merits of Christ's cross as a justification for sinning—in this case, lying, the Eighth Commandment (or, for Protestants, the Ninth) notwithstanding.

5) The Eucharist is, without question, the most holy, precious, valuable, and sublime gift that our Lord Jesus Christ has given to us. St. Ignatius calls the body and blood of Christ "love incorruptible" (Letter to the Romans 7:3), which, as St. Bernard of Clairvaux describes it, "surpasses all loves in heaven and on earth."

"Let everyone be struck with fear," St. Francis of Assisi declares, "when Christ, the Son of the living God, is present on the altar in the hands of a priest!" Quotations like these from the most august of the Catholic Church's saints could be multiplied many times over . . . and yet Martin Luther seems less than impressed.

Some context and a little history here will be helpful to better understand the issues involved.

Luther felt that the Eucharist as instituted by Christ was rather simple: the communion of bread and wine. He claimed that over the course of time, Rome corrupted the Mass by adding all kinds of unwanted and superfluous things that detracted from the central element of the Eucharist:

> We cannot deny that the mass, i.e., the communion of bread and wine, is a rite divinely instituted by Christ himself and that it was observed first by Christ and then by the apostles, quite simply and evangelically without any additions. But in the course of time so many human inventions were added to it that nothing except the names of the mass and communion has come down to us.[124]

Luther's claim does not really square with the facts. The Canon of the Mass was developing and maturing, and although language and the arrangement of prayers and names have changed over the centuries, the substance of the Canon has nonetheless remained largely intact.

All the way back in the second century (around the year 155), St. Justin Martyr wrote to the pagan emperor Antoninus Pius and gave him a basic summary of what happens at Mass:

> On the day we call the day of the sun, all who dwell in the city or country gather in the same place. The memoirs of the apostles and the writings of the prophets are read, as much as time permits. When the reader has finished, he who presides over those

> gathered admonishes and challenges them to imitate these beautiful things.
>
> Then we all rise together and offer prayers for ourselves . . . and for all others, wherever they may be, so that we may be found righteous by our life and actions, and faithful to the commandments, so as to obtain eternal salvation.
>
> When the prayers are concluded we exchange the kiss. Then someone brings bread and a cup of water and wine mixed together to him who presides over the brethren. He takes them and offers praise and glory to the Father of the universe, through the name of the Son and of the Holy Spirit and for a considerable time he gives thanks (in Greek: *eucharistia*) that we have been judged worthy of these gifts.
>
> When he has concluded the prayers and thanksgivings, all present give voice to an acclamation by saying, "Amen." When he who presides has given thanks and the people have responded, those whom we call deacons give to those present the "eucharisted" bread, wine, and water and take them to those who are absent (CCC 1345).[125]

Anyone familiar with the Mass will instantly recognize what Justin is talking about, because this same content is still in place today. Nothing of substance has changed in the Mass for a very long time. In the thousand years from the end of the fourth century to the fourteenth century, for example, only "minor changes, clarifications, and adjustments took place in the words of the Canon and the gestures that accompanied it."[126] The *Catholic Encyclopedia* notes, "It may be taken for certain that in the time of St. Gregory I (590-604) the Canon already stood as it does now"—1,300 years later at the time of this article—and

> certainly when St. Gregory became pope our Canon was already fixed in its present order. There are scarcely any changes to note in its history since then. "No pope has added to or changed the Canon since St. Gregory," says Benedict XIV [reigned 1740-1758] (*De SS. Missæ Sacr.*, 162).[127]

What Luther derided as "additions" are ancient in origin and were instituted by the Church to reflect the fullness of what true worship is: recall the Father's saving activity in Christ, offer a prayer of thanksgiving to the Father, call down the Holy Spirit upon the bread and wine to transform them, remember both the living and the dead, acknowledge saintly men and women (in the Roman Canon), offer intercessions for the faithful, and present it all to the Father in the name of Christ, whose sacrifice the Mass is. Like Church doctrine, Church worship matured over time, but the Mass of Luther's day was in essence the same as it is today.

Considering the content of the Canon, it's difficult to imagine what part of it a self-professed Christian could find objectionable or offensive.

For Catholics, the words "Mass" and "Eucharist" are effectively synonyms. We do not create an artificial distinction between the two, the way Luther did. It is at Mass where the Eucharist is consecrated, and all the activities of the Mass lead to the sacrificial offering of Jesus' body and blood under the appearance of bread and wine (and water).

With this understanding in mind, we can better appreciate what the saints had to say about the Mass. Here are a few examples.

> "When the Mass is being celebrated, the sanctuary is filled with countless angels, who adore the divine Victim immolated on the altar."
>
> —St. John Chrysostom (347-407), bishop, Doctor of the Church

> "One merits more devoutly by assisting at a Holy Mass than by distributing all of his goods to the poor and traveling all over the world on pilgrimage."
>
> —St. Bernard of Clairvaux (1090-1153), abbot, mystic, co-founder of the Knights Templar

> "The celebration of Holy Mass has the same value as the death of Jesus on the cross."
>
> —St. Francis of Assisi (1183-1224), stigmatist, mystic, and founder of the Franciscans

> "No human tongue can enumerate the favors that trace back to the sacrifice of the Mass. The sinner is reconciled with God; the just man becomes more upright; sins are wiped away; vices are uprooted; virtue and merit increase; and the devil's schemes are frustrated."
>
> —St. Lawrence Justinian (1381-1456), bishop and first patriarch of Venice

> "Here on earth it's impossible to perform a more meritorious act than visiting Jesus often in the Eucharist. If you took all of the good works done by all of the humans who have ever lived in all of history and stacked them all up and multiplied them by a million, they wouldn't equal the merit, the virtue and the worth of one Mass."
>
> —St. Teresa of Ávila (1515-1582), Doctor of the Church, mystic

> "Know, O Christian, that the Mass is the holiest act of religion. You cannot do anything to glorify God more, nor profit your soul more, than by devoutly assisting at it, and assisting as often as possible.
>
> —St. Peter Julian Eymard (1811-1868), priest, founder of two religious institutes

> "O what awesome mysteries take place during Mass! . . . One day we will know what God is doing for us in each Mass and what sort of gift he is preparing in it for us. Only his divine love could permit that such a gift be provided for us . . . this foundation of life gushing forth with such sweetness and power."
>
> —St. Faustina Kowalska (1905-1938), nun, mystic

> "It would be easier for the world to survive without the sun than to do so without the Holy Mass."
>
> —St. Padre Pio (1887-1968), priest, stigmatist

In stark and troubling opposition to these words and sentiments is what Luther said about the Mass. I hesitate to relay his words, but I think it is necessary. The quotes could easily be multiplied, but several representative examples will suffice for our purposes.

> In the things which are "musts" and are matters of necessity, such as believing in Christ, love nevertheless uses force or undue constraint. Thus the mass is an evil thing, and God is displeased with it, because it is performed as if it were a sacrifice and work of merit. Therefore it must be abolished.[128]

> That the Mass in the papacy must be the greatest and most horrible abomination, as it directly and powerfully conflicts with this chief article ("That Jesus Christ, our God and Lord, died for our sins, and was raised again for our justification" [Rom. 4:25]), and yet above and before all other popish idolatries it has been the chief and most specious. For it has been held that this sacrifice or work of the Mass, even though it be rendered by a wicked scoundrel, frees men from sins, both in this life and also in purgatory, while only the Lamb of God shall and must do this.[129]

> No man can make the papists believe that the private mass is the greatest blaspheming of God, and the highest idolatry upon earth, an abomination the like to which has never been in Christendom since the time of the apostles; for they are blinded and hardened therein, so that their understanding and knowledge of God, and of all divine matters, is perverted and erroneous. They hold that to be the most upright and greatest service of God, which, in truth, is the greatest and most abominable idolatry.[130]

> I really wish and would very gladly see and hear that everybody would recognize the difference between the two words "Mass" and "sacrament" to be as great as the difference between darkness and light, nay, between the devil and God, since the Mass, as its performance and all their teachings and books prove, is nothing else than a perverted disorder and a marketing of the Holy sacrament, even though it be celebrated in the most devotional manner. . . . God grant all pious Christians such a heart that they are afraid to cross themselves, as against an abomination of the devil, when they hear the word "Mass."[131]

> That God has been able to put up with this [abomination of the Mass] so long is one of my great surprises. Such patience is beyond comprehension.[132]

> The abomination of the Mass no tongue can express, no heart can adequately [*digne*] appreciate. It would not have been surprising [*murum*] if God had destroyed the entire world because of it, just as the pope has certainly destroyed a large part of the world by the traffic of the Mass. But when he comes with the fire of Judgment Day, he will give him an adequate reward.[133]

These two respective views on the Mass—the saints' versus Luther's—are diametrically opposed. Clearly, they cannot both be accurate. One of them has to be seriously in error.

"*Nemo Dat Quod Non Habet*"

This Latin saying translates literally as, "No one gives what he doesn't have." It originated in a legal context, but its application extends far beyond legal considerations. It is axiomatic that I cannot extend to others what I myself lack—intellectually, morally, emotionally, physically, and spiritually speaking. For example,

- I cannot teach others how to do algebra if I don't understand it myself.
- I cannot engender in others a peaceful spirit if my own is restless.
- I cannot teach someone a skill (e.g., glassblowing, painting, or carpentry) that I don't master.
- I cannot effectively counsel or lead others in the spiritual life if I myself do not have a living relationship with Christ.
- I cannot teach others how to grow in virtue and holiness if have not cultivated them in my own life.
- I cannot exhort others to verbal restraint and temperance if I cannot control my own tongue and temperament.

With Luther, there is an important application of this saying. His spirit was so disquieted, his attitude so angry, his words so caustic, his behavior so rebellious, his influence so destructive, his hatred so all-encompassing, and the fruits of his labors so rotten that it is difficult to conceive how he was in a position to reform anything, let alone an institution as significant as Christ's

Church. True reform in the Church—ever necessary because of the presence of sin in human beings!—has always come from its saintly members, who gave to the Church what they themselves possessed: an inwardly renewed spirit and a transformed heart. Such people clearly took to heart Jesus' counsel:

> Why do you notice the splinter in your brother's eye, but do not perceive the wooden beam in your own eye? How can you say to your brother, 'Let me remove that splinter from your eye,' while the wooden beam is in your eye? You hypocrite, *remove the wooden beam from your eye first*; then you will see clearly to remove the splinter from your brother's eye (Matt. 7:3-5).

What Luther did was the opposite of the Latin saying: he gave what he did not possess. How could it be otherwise?

Pope Leo X, noted above as the reigning pontiff at the time and the one who formally condemned Luther's *Ninety-five Theses* in the bull *Exsurge Domine*, had the following to say:

> For we can scarcely express, from distress and grief of mind, what has reached our ears for some time by the report of reliable men and general rumor; alas, we have even seen with our eyes and read the many diverse errors. Some of these have already been condemned by councils and the constitutions of our predecessors, and expressly contain even the heresy of the Greeks and Bohemians. Other errors are either heretical, false, scandalous, or offensive to pious ears, as seductive of simple minds, originating with false exponents of the faith who in their proud curiosity

> yearn for the world's glory, and contrary to the apostle's teaching, wish to be wiser than they should be.

After referring to Luther's errors as "pernicious poison," the pope goes on to list forty-one errors, which he says are only "some" of them. Then he says,

> No one of sound mind is ignorant how destructive, pernicious, scandalous, and seductive to pious and simple minds these various errors are, how opposed they are to all charity and reverence for the holy Roman Church who is the mother of all the faithful and teacher of the faith; how destructive they are of the vigor of ecclesiastical discipline, namely obedience. This virtue is the font and origin of all virtues and without it anyone is readily convicted of being unfaithful.

Sufficient Grace

It is said that God gives every person sufficient grace to attain heaven. This is no less true for Luther. Despite his troubled conscience, scrupulous spirit, volatile temperament, and emotional upheavals, Luther experienced multiple moments of clarity, when God's grace broke through the darkness and confusion in his heart.

> How often has my heart been tantalized, how often has it punished me and reproached me with their [the "papists'"] only strongest argument: Are you alone wise? Can it be supposed that all others have erred, and erred so long a time? What if you should

> be mistaken and should lead many into error, who would be eternally damned?[134]

The Holy Spirit spoke to Luther's conscience and told him *exactly* what he needed to hear. It wasn't the first time, either. Luther says these thoughts came to him "often." They are also in substance the same thing John Eck said to him at the Diet of Worms in 1521—which, for Luther, was the point of no return.

God was attempting to hold Luther back from the spiritual precipice upon which he was standing, trying to keep him from jumping off. However, God does not redeem us against our will, nor will he bend our wills to his purposes, even though heaven is the goal. We are truly free.

Sadly, Martin Luther fell prey to his own ego and invented a veneer of divine approval. He was so convinced of his own righteousness and his own cause that he made Scripture say what he wanted—and *needed*—it to say:

> Thus I felt until Christ fortified and confirmed me with his only certain Word, so that now my heart is uneasy no longer, but resists this argument of the papists, as a stony shore resists the waves, and ridicules their threats and fury.[135]

Scripture warns us in stark and incisive terms about the corruption of the human heart. This is why our own judgment *must* be measured against something external, something that is *not* self-serving. Luther engaged in another Michal's game: in the same way Michal dressed up a series of objects to look like the future king David, Luther twisted the scriptures to validate his rebellion against Christ's Church.

As the book of Genesis teaches us (and the Psalms, and Ecclesiastes, and Romans, and . . .), enthroning the ego is the fundamental sin of the human race. We must not be surprised, therefore, that the masses were receptive to Luther's call to revert to the original rebellion in the Garden of Eden. Tragically, it is in our spiritual DNA.

EGO ENTHRONED

Behold, I was brought forth in iniquity, and in sin did my mother conceive me (Ps. 51:5).

Surely there is not a righteous man on earth who does good and never sins. (Eccles. 7:20).

For I know that nothing good dwells within me, that is, my flesh. I can will what is right, but I cannot do it. For I do not do the good I want, but the evil I do not want is what I do (Rom. 7:18-19).

It takes hard, committed, sustained work through God's grace to overcome our fallen nature, to resist sin and temptation, and to grow in virtue and holiness (Phil. 2:12–13). It is far easier to feed into our passions and resist moving out of our spiritual comfort zones, because doing so resonates with our sinful nature.

In what is simultaneously perhaps the worst tragedy and irony, Luther once noted,

> Heretics cannot themselves appear good unless they depict the Church as evil, false, and mendacious. They alone wish to be esteemed as the good, but the Church must be made to appear evil in every respect.[136]

Luther sums up his rebellion against Jesus' Church in this simple statement. And although he railed against the Church with such ferocity and with such untiring effort that he succeeded—in some people's eyes—in making the Church appear exactly this way, the underlying reality, apparently lost on him, is that this is how heretics accomplish their goals.

What Might Have Been

Sometimes it is fruitless to ponder what *might have* been, since the reality of what *actually is* remains indisputable and static. At other times, it is an interesting and even productive intellectual pursuit to imagine the *what if* had circumstances been different. Such a pursuit could lead to better future results by considering more possibilities. Along these lines, let's think about the following. Imagine if Luther . . .

. . . had taken his iron will, his theological education, his monastic experience, his writing skill, and his determination to set things right and used them *within the Church* to effect a true reformation.

. . . had set such a compelling example of holiness and virtue that others could not help but follow it.

. . . had disciplined himself and mastered his passions so effectively that people would flock to him to learn how to do likewise.

. . . had dedicated his untiring efforts to renewing Christ's Church instead of fomenting rebellion against it.

. . . had imitated the likes of Francis of Assisi, Catherine of Siena, and Francisco Ximénes de Cisneros and brought true reform to the Church.

We can only wonder what the result might have looked like. But it is reasonable to assume that it would have been amazing.

EPILOGUE

Jesus is the groom of his mystical body, the Church (Rev. 21:1-2, 9-10). It is inconceivable that he would ever have allowed his spouse to fall so far away from the truth, to distort his teachings so badly that they would become unrecognizable, to become so corrupt and sinful while on the Holy Spirit's watch, to become so distant from him, that someone needed to bring the Church back from the brink of sanity.

Instead, it makes far more sense to take Jesus' promises to safeguard his Church at face value and to trust him to keep those promises, even in the face of human sinfulness—agenda, treachery, lawlessness, rebellion, egoism, pride, and a host of other transgressions we may rightly call *legion*, because "we are many." When has God ever allowed sin to stand in the way of bringing about his plan of redemption? From the start in the Garden of Eden, in the midst of human rebellion and the rupturing of their relationship with God, the *protoevangelium*—the foreshadowing of his plan to save us—was *already present* (see Gen. 3:15).

The Old Testament points to and is centered on Jesus Christ. There are multiple images of Christ's Church in both the Old and New Testaments. Jesus' Church was big news, and prefigured in many ways (see, for instance, CCC 753-762). In fact, the *Catechism* goes so far as to say that the Church is "a plan born in the Father's heart," and that it was "foreshadowed from the world's beginning" (headings for 759 and 760) It even calls Christ's Church "the goal of all things" (760).

With these thoughts in mind, and having presented the fundamental flaws of *sola scriptura*, I invite the reader to consider one last series of questions:

1. With so much prefiguring and preparation, how could it be claimed that Christ's Church fell so far from its founder?

2. How could Christians not only believe, but *accept and affirm* that such a thing actually happened? It is preposterous enough to suggest that Jesus had been remiss in keeping his promise to be with his Church and that the Holy Spirit was negligent in his duty to guard the Church's indefectibility, but isn't it even more absurd to suggest that Martin Luther succeeded where Jesus and the Holy Spirit had failed?

3. Jesus perfectly fulfilled the Father's will and brought his Church into existence as the universal means of salvation for the human race (Matt. 28:18-20). Could Jesus have been

so careless as to allow his bride to become doctrinally corrupted to the point of "losing the gospel"?

4. Could the Holy Spirit, whom Jesus explicitly sent to remind the apostles of everything he taught them and to be the Church's guarantor of truth, fail in his mission?

5. How could the Catholic Church's teachings have become so corrupted if you can see that its teachings are the same, albeit matured and developed over time, in every century for the past 2,000 years? Wouldn't you instead expect to see a point where doctrines began to deviate?

6. How can *sola scriptura*, which has no historical continuity, no biblical precedent, and no prefiguring like what the Church has, be the sole rule of faith for Christians? Doesn't the Father always announce his intentions?

7. If *sola scriptura* is as central to the life of the Church as Protestants claim, why was it not foretold by the prophets, practiced in the Old Testament, affirmed as the sole rule of faith for God's covenant people, explicitly taught by Jesus, spread by the teachings of the apostles, repeatedly affirmed throughout the writings of the early Church Fathers, and clearly delineated in the Church's important creeds?

ABOUT THE AUTHOR

Joel S. Peters is a frequent contributor to *Catholic Answers Magazine*. He has forty-five years of experience in multiple areas of Church ministry. He has been a Catholic high school theology teacher for more than twenty-five years and has also worked for many years as a campus minister. He has a master's degree from Immaculate Conception Seminary at Seton Hall University and a catechist certification from the Newark Archdiocese. He enjoys reading, travel, history, and photography.

ENDNOTES

1 See, for instance, the *Joint Declaration on the Doctrine of Justification*, a document signed by the Catholic Church and the Lutheran World Federation on October 31, 1999. For additional examples of the Catholic Church's efforts to promote Christian unity, see the Pontifical Council for Promoting Christian unity at http://www.christianunity.va/content/unitacristiani/en/dialoghi. html.

2 Some scholars now question whether this actually happened. See the History.com article at https://www.history.com/news/martin-luther-might-not-have-nailed-his-95-theses-to-the-church-door, accessed April 13, 2024.

3 *The Formula of Concord*, Solid Declaration (1577), Comprehensive Summary, Foundation, Rule and Norm 1, Book of Concord Online, https://bookofconcord.org/solid-declaration. The brackets are in the original. I have added italics for emphasis.

4 St. Francis de Sales, *The Catholic Controversy* (Charlotte, NC: TAN Books, 1989), 112.

5 "Luther at the Imperial Diet of Worms (1521)," https://www.luther.de/en/worms.html, accessed on April 12, 2024.

6 James R. White, *Scripture Alone: Exploring the Bible's Accuracy, Authority, and Authenticity* (Minneapolis, MN: Bethany House Publishers, 2004), 27.

7 Jimmy Akin, "What Exactly Do You Mean by Sola Scriptura?", Catholic Answers Magazine, July 1, 2005, https://www.catholic.com/magazine/print-edition/what-exactly-do-you-mean-by-sola-scriptura, accessed April 13, 2024.

8 Tim Staples, "According to Scripture: Why the 'Bible Alone' is an Unworkable Rule of Faith," *Catholic Answers Magazine*, January 1, 2007, https://www.catholic.com/magazine/print-edition/according-to-scripture, accessed on April 13, 2024.

9 James White, in a debate with Patrick Madrid, September 28, 1993. The transcript of this debate can be found on White's website at https://www.aomin.org/aoblog/roman-catholicism/does-the-bible-teach-sola-scriptura, accessed on April 13, 2024.

10 Charles Spurgeon, "Salvation by Knowing the Truth" (Sermon No. 1506), given at the Metropolitan Tabernacle in Newington (South London, England). The transcript is found at https://www.blueletterbible.org/Comm/spurgeon_charles/sermons/1516.cfm, accessed on April 13, 2024.

11 Norman L. Geisler and Ralph E. MacKenzie, "What is Sola Scriptura," Christian Research Institute, April 8, 2009, https://www.equip.org/articles/what-is-sola-scriptura, accessed on April 13, 2024.

12 Zondervan Academic Blog, "What Is Sola Scriptura?", August 2, 2018, https://zondervanacademic.com/blog/what-is-sola-scriptura, accessed on April 13, 2024.

13 Marty Foord, "The Real Meaning of Sola Scriptura," The Gospel Coalition, Australia Edition, August 25, 2017, https://au.thegospelcoalition.org/article/the-real-meaning-of-sola-scriptura, accessed on April 13, 2024.

14 Robert M. Bowman Jr. "Understanding *Sola Scriptura*: The Evangelical View of the Authority of the Bible," Institute for Religious Research, February 1, 2018, https://bib.irr.org/understanding-sola-scriptura-evangelical-view-of-authority-of-bible, accessed on April 13, 2024.

15 Jimmy Akin, *The Bible is a Catholic Book* (El Cajon, CA: Catholic Answers Press, 2019), 172-173.

16 Right Rev. Henry G. Graham, *Where We Got the Bible: Our Debt to the Catholic Church*, (Rockford, IL: TAN Books and Publishers, Inc., 1977), 38-39.

17 "The Tercentenary of a True Reformer" (no author listed), *The Month: A Catholic Magazine and Review*, Vol. LII, September – December 1884, London: Burns & Oates, 489-490, taken from https://books.google.com/books?id=6AMFAAAAQAAJ, italics in original. The quote may have originally come from Johann Georg Walch's edition of *Luther's Works*, Vol. XIII, 2,195. Note: The "True Reformer" in the article's title refers to St. Charles Borromeo, not Martin Luther.

18 Graham, 34-35.

19 White, 100.

20 James Swan, "Sproul: 'The Bible is a fallible collection of infallible books," Beggars All website, February 9, 2011, https://beggarsallreformation.blogspot.com/2011/02/sproul-bible-is-fallible-collection-of.html, accessed on April 15, 2024.

21 White, 46.

22 Taken from https://www.usccb.org/prayers/nicene-creed.

23 William Barry, "Arius," *The Catholic Encyclopedia*, Vol. 1 (New York: Robert Appleton Company, 1907), http://www.newadvent.org/cathen/01718a.htm, accessed on April 24, 2024.

24 For example, he cited Proverbs 8:22-25, Mark 10:18, John 14:28 and 17:3, and 1 Timothy 6:15-16, to name a few passages. See his letter to Alexander (bishop of Alexandria) circa 320. See also https://christianity.stackexchange.com/questions/36586/what-scriptures-did-arius-use-to-support-teaching-that-jesus-was-created.

25 Taken from https://www.ccel.org/creeds/athanasian.creed.html.

26 Christian Classics Ethereal Library, https://www.ccel.org/creeds/chalcedonian-creed.html, accessed on April 15, 2024. The brackets are in the original.

27 John Calvin, *Commentary on Corinthians, Volume 1*, Christian Classics Ethereal Library, https://www.ccel.org/ccel/calvin/calcom39.xi.ii.html, accessed on April 15, 2024.

28 Karlo Broussard. *Meeting the Protestant Challenge: How to Answer 50 Biblical Objections to Catholic Beliefs* (El Cajon, CA: Catholic Answers Press, 2019), 60-61.

29 *Strong's Exhaustive Concordance of the Bible* (with Hebrew and Greek lexicon), word 3956, https://biblehub.com/greek/3956.htm, accessed on April 15, 2024.

30 *Strong's Concordance*. See word 5624, *óphelimos*, https://biblehub.com/str/greek/5624.htm.

31 *Strong's Concordance*, word 975, https://biblehub.com/str/greek/975.htm, accessed on April 15, 2024.

32 Nathan Busenitz, "Sola Scriptura and the Church Fathers," The Master's Seminary Blog, June 9, 2015, https://blog.tms.edu/sola-scriptura-and-the-church-fathers, accessed on April 15, 2024.

33 *Ibid*.

34 Harold O.J. Brown, *Heresies* (Peabody, MA: Hendrickson Publishers, 1988), 97.

35 See Eusebius's account of the controversy in his *Church History*, book 3, chapters 23-25 at https://earlychurchtexts.com/public/eusebius_quartodeciman_controversy.htm, accessed on April 15, 2024.

36 Roland H. Bainton, *Here I Stand: A Life of Martin Luther* (New York: Abingdon-Cokesbury Press, 1950), 185.

37 Hartmann Grisar, S.J., *Martin Luther: His Life and Work*, Arthur Preuss, ed. (Westminster, MD: The Newman Press, 1961), 187.

38 Martin Luther, James C. Galvin, ed. *Faith Alone: A Daily Devotional* (Grand Rapids, MI: Zondervan, 2009), entry for July 2.

39 For an illustrative, but not exhaustive, list of heresies the Church has condemned, see Catholic Answers' tract, "The Great Heresies," at https://www.catholic.com/tract/the-great-heresies, accessed on April 15, 2024.

40 Graham, 31.

41 See Stuart A.P. Murray, *The Library: An Illustrated History* (New York: Skyhorse Publishing, 2009), 31.

42 Raymond F. Collins, *Introduction to the New Testament* (Garden City, NY: Doubleday & Company, Inc., 1983), 77.

43 *Id.*, 100-102.

44 Bruce M. Metzger, *The Text of the New Testament: Its Transmission, Corruption, and Restoration* (Oxford University Press, 1992), 221-225, 234-242.

45 *Id.*, 226-228.

46 See the footnote for Mark 16:9-20 in the New American Bible.

47 Collins, 102.

48 Metzger, 234.

49 Hershel Shanks, *The Dead Sea Scrolls—Discovery and Meaning*, Biblical Archaeology Society, 2007, 7.

50 Ed Stetzer, "Why the Dead Sea Scrolls Are Significant," Apostolic Information Service, Indiana Bible College, August 11, 2007, https://www.apostolic.edu/why-the-dead-sea-scrolls-are-significant/, accessed on April 15, 2024.

51 See the article at Biblica, https://www.biblica.com/resources/bible-faqs/why-does-the-niv-bible-omit-or-have-missing-verses, accessed on April 15, 2024.

52 Jimmy Akin, "Practical Problems of Sola Scriptura," https://jimmyakin.com/library/practical-problems-of-sola-scriptura, accessed on April 15, 2024.

53 Biblica, Bible FAQs, "How was the Bible distributed before the printing press was invented in 1455?", https://www.biblica.com, accessed on April 15, 2024.

54 See https://www.codexsinaiticus.org/en/codex/default.aspx.

55 Kurt and Barbara Aland, *The Text of the New Testament: An Introduction to the Critical Editions and to the Theory and Practice of Modern Textual Criticism* (Grand Rapids, MI: William B. Eerdmans, 1987), 77.

56 Philip Hughes, *A Popular History of the Reformation* (Garden City, NY: Hanover House, 1957), 14, footnote 3.

57 James M. Arlandson, "Basic Facts on Producing New Testament Manuscripts," August 31, 2015, https://bible.org/seriespage/2-basic-facts-producing-new-testament-manuscripts, accessed on April 15, 2024.

58 James Arlandson, "New Testament Manuscripts: The Right Stuff," February 11, 2007, https://www.americanthinker.com/articles/2007/02/new_testament_manuscripts_the_1.html, accessed on April 15, 2024.

59 Evan Andrews, "7 Things You May Not Know About the Gutenberg Bible," September 5, 2023, https://www.history.com/news/7-things-you-may-not-know-about-the-gutenberg-bible, accessed on April 15, 2024.

60 Murray, 39.

61 *Id.*, 35.

62 "Differences between Parchment, Vellum, and Paper," National Archives, August 15, 2016, https://www.archives.gov/preservation/formats/paper-vellum.html, accessed on April 17, 2024.

63 Bruce Metzger, "For most of its long history, the Bible was copied by hand. How easy was it for a mistake to enter into this process?" Christian Bible Studies, June 28, 2011, https://www.christianitytoday.com/biblestudies/bible-answers/theology/biblecopiedhand.html, accessed on April 17, 2024.

64 Murray, 35, and Kenneth Hodges, "List Price of Medieval Items," https://medieval.ucdavis.edu/120D/Money.html, accessed on April 17, 2024.

65 Victoria Corwin, "Medieval Book Production and Monastic Life," Dartmouth College, Dartmouth Ancient Books Lab, May 24, 2016, https://sites.dartmouth.edu/ancientbooks/2016/ 05/24/medieval-book-production-and-monastic-life, accessed on April 17, 2024.

66 David Flusser et al., "Biblical Literature," *Encyclopedia Britannica*, August 20, 2020, https://www.britannica.com/topic/biblical-literature/Types-of-writing-materials-and-methods, accessed on April 17, 2024.

67 Jehovah's Witnesses Official Website, New World Translation, online Study Edition, 2019, https://www.jw.org/en/library/bible/study-bible/books/luke/23, accessed on April 17, 2024.

68 Hughes, 14.

69 Max Roser and Esteban Ortiz-Ospina, "Literacy," https://ourworldindata.org/literacy, first published in 2013 and revised in March 2024, accessed on April 17, 2024.

70 See https://www.biblegateway.com/passage/?search=John%20 2&version=NET, footnote (g).

71 Bernard Ward, "Cana," *The Catholic Encyclopedia*, Vol. 3 (New York: Robert Appleton Company, 1908), http://www.newadvent.org/cathen/03226a.htm, accessed on April 17, 2024.

72 See the Greek Interlinear at https://biblehub.com/interlinear/john/2-4.htm.

73 "The Wedding at Cana," Institute of Catholic Culture, https://instituteofcatholicculture.org/articles/the-luminous-mysteries-part-three, accessed on April 17, 2024.

74 Though this quote has been ascribed to St. Augustine, it originated with an early seventeenth-century Lutheran theologian, Rupertus Meldenius. See Georgetown University Professor James J. O'Donnell's treatment of the origins of the quote at https://faculty.georgetown.edu/jod/augustine/quote.html, accessed on April 17, 2024.

75 The quote is attributed to Alistair Begg, an American Evangelical Protestant pastor and the voice behind "Truth for Life," a weekly radio program.

76 White, 86. All italics are in the original.

77 For a rich and comprehensive understanding of this discourse in particular, see Brant Pitre's book, *Jesus and the Jewish Roots of the Eucharist: Unlocking the Secrets of the Last Supper* (New York: Doubleday, 2016), especially Chapter 4: The Manna of the Messiah.

78 Footnote for verse 53 in the *New American Bible*.

79 Rev. Jonathan Krenz, "How the Formula of Concord Came to Be," August 8, 2017, https://resources.lcms.org/reading-study/how-the-formula-of-concord-came-to-be/, accessed on April 17, 2024.

80 Steve Weidenkopf, *20 Answers: The Reformation*. (El Cajon, CA: Catholic Answers Press, 2017), 8. Weidenkopf quotes Hilaire Belloc, *The Great Heresies*, published by TAN Books and Publishing, Inc., 1991, 110.

81 Jimmy Akin. *20 Answers: Faith & Works* (El Cajon, CA: Catholic Answers Press, 2020), 7-10. All italics are in the original, whereas the ellipses are mine.

82 *Luther's Werke*, Weimar, 1898, 5:407, 35 and Weimar, 1833, 5:407.

83 Martin Luther, Address to the Nobility of the German Nation (1520), Fordham University, Modern History Sourcebook: Martin Luther (1483-1546), https://sourcebooks.fordham.edu/mod/luther-nobility.asp, accessed on April 17, 2024.

84 Msgr. Patrick O'Hare, *The Facts About Luther* (Rockford, IL: TAN Books and Publishers, Inc., 1987), 141.

85 Westminster Confession of Faith, Chapter 1, Number 7, https://www.ligonier.org/learn/articles/westminster-confession-faith, accessed on April 17, 2024.

86 Jansen, Vol. III, p. 84, as quoted in O'Hare, 51.

87 "What is OCD & Scrupulosity?", International OCD Foundation, https://iocdf.org/faith-ocd/what-is-ocd-scrupulosity/, accessed on April 17, 2024.

88 Martin Luther, quoted in Bainton, 41. Note that this was Luther's frame of mind as a result of saying his *first* Mass.

89 Bainton, 54.

90 Martin Luther, *Commentary on the Epistle to the Galatians*, 1535, Chapter 5, Verse 3, http://www.projectwittenberg.org/pub/resources/text/wittenberg/luther/gal/gal5-01.txt, accessed on April 17, 2024.

91 Father Peter Stravinskas, ed., *Catholic Encyclopedia* (Huntington, Indiana: Our Sunday Visitor, Inc., 1991), 873.

92 "Martin Luther," OCDUK, https://www.ocduk.org/ocd/history-of-ocd/martin-luther, accessed on April 17, 2024.

93 "Who Was Martin Luther?" (no author listed), https://www.bibleinfo.com/en/questions/who-was-martin-luther, accessed on April 17, 2024.

94 Henry Ganss, "Martin Luther," *The Catholic Encyclopedia*, Vol 9. (New York: Robert Appleton Company, 1910), https://www.newadvent.org/cathen/09438b.htm, accessed on April 17, 2024.

95 "Anfechtung and Absolution Part 1," The American Association of Lutheran Churches, October 27, 2014, https://www.taalc.org/blog/post/anfechtung-and-absolution-part-1, accessed on April 17, 2024.

96 Grisar, 200, 204.

97 George T. Deas, "Martin Luther: Hero, But No Saint," *America* magazine, April 25, 2017, https://www.americamagazine.org/arts-culture/2017/04/25/martin-luther-hero-no-saint, accessed on April 17, 2024.

98 "Martin Luther: The Characters," entry on Luther's parents, https://www.pbs.org/empires/martinluther/char_parents.html, accessed on April 17, 2024.

99 Algis Valiunas, "Martin Luther's Reformation: The First Protestant," Fall 2017, https:// claremontreviewofbooks.com/martin-luthers-reformation, accessed on April 17, 2024.

100 "Highlights of Luther's Life" (no author listed), https://www.christianity.com/church/church-history/timeline/1201-1500/highlights-of-luthers-life-11629892.html, August 21 ,2023, accessed on April 17, 2024. The ellipsis is in the original. Where this source reads, ". . . and came to bear a grudge against him," other sources of the quote use more emphatic language such as, "I hated him until he finally . . ." The "grudge" translation may be an attempt to soften the impact of Luther's words. A grudge and hatred are rather different realities.

101 R.C. Sproul, "The Insanity of Luther," https://www.ligonier.org/learn/series/holiness-of-god/the-insanity-of-luther, accessed on April 17, 2024. An internet search reveals several Protestant websites that reference or link this video or transcript of Sproul's talk. It would seem that Sproul is not alone in thinking the way he does about Luther's "insanity."

102 Quoted in Right Rev. John Milner, *Letters on the Rule of Faith; or the Method of Finding Out the True Religion* (London: P. & M. Andrews, 1838), Tract 4, page 17. Milner identifies only "Visit. Saxon." as the source of the quote.

103 Weidenkopf, 37-38.

104 Papal Encyclicals Online, https://www.papalencyclicals.net/leo10/l10exdom.htm, accessed on April 17, 2024. Both quotes are taken from the first paragraph of the bull.

105 Dr. Michael Chamberlain, "Are Wild Boars Dangerous? How, When, and Why They Attack," https://rangerplanet.com/are-wild-boars-dangerous-how-when-why-they-attack, accessed on April 17, 2024.

106 Glenna F. McGregor et al. "Disease risk associated with free-ranging wild boar in Saskatchewan," *The Canadian Veterinary Journal* 2015 August; 56(8): 839-844. Taken from the National Center for Biotechnology Information, a division of the National Institutes of Health, https://www.ncbi.nlm.nih.gov/pmc/articles/PMC4502852, accessed on April 17, 2024.

107 Written to Spalatin and quoted in Bainton, 160.

108 Robert Kolb, "Luther's Truths, Then and Now," Concordia Theology, May 6, 2015, https://concordiatheology.org/2015/05/luthers-truths-then-and-now, accessed on April 17, 2024.

109 Katharina Von Bora, Lutherland, https://www.luther-land.com/en/w/katharina-von-bora-luther, accessed on April 17, 2024.

110 Dr. Lyndal Roper, *Martin Luther: Renegade and Prophet* (New York: Random House, 2016), p. xxv.

111 Dr. Mark U. Edwards, Jr., "After the Revolution," Christian History Institute, https://christianhistoryinstitute.org/magazine/article/after-the-revolution, accessed on April 17, 2024. The website notes, "Christian History originally published this article in *Christian History* Issue #39 in 1993."

112 Diane V. Bowers, "To Spite the Devil: Martin Luther and Katharina von Bora's Wedding as Reform and Resistance," *Religions* 2020, *11*(3), 116, https://www.mdpi.com/2077-1444/11/3/116, accessed on April 17, 2024.

113 Quoted in Grisar, 442.

114 Weidenkopf, 15-16.

115 See *Christianity Today*, https://www.christianitytoday.com/history/people/theologians/martin-luther.html, accessed on April 17, 2024. The website says that this article came from the book *131 Christians Everyone Should Know*, by the editors of *Christian History* magazine, Nashville, TN: Broadman & Holman Publishers, 2000.

116 Grisar, 259-260.

117 Sproul, "The Insanity of Luther."

118 Phillip Cary, "Martin Luther Battles the Devil," The Great Courses Daily, August 11, 2017. Available at the Internet Archive: https://web.archive.org/web/20211010024950/https:/www.thegreatcoursesdaily.com/luther-battle-devil, accessed April 24, 2024.

119 Dr. Mark U. Edwards, Jr., "After the Revolution," Christian History Institute, originally published (according to the website) in *Christian History*, Issue 39, 1993. See https://christianhistoryinstitute.org/magazine/article/after-the-revolution, accessed on April 17, 2024.

120 *Ibid.*

121 "Philipp, Landgrave of Hesse," Reformation 500, https://reformation500.csl.edu/bio/philipp-i-landgrave-of-hesse, accessed on April 17, 2024.

122 Grisar, 522. Grisar cites his own more extensive work on Luther as the source: *Luther*, Vol. IV, 51. He adds, "Excerpted from Philip's *Briefwechsel*, ed. by Lenz, pp. 373, 375."

123 *Ibid.*

124 *Luther's Works*, Vol. 53: Liturgy and Hymns. Ulrich S. Leupold and Helmut T. Lehman, eds., Philadelphia: Fortress Press, 1965, 20.

125 The original text is from St. Justin's *First Apology*, 65-67: PG 6,428-429. *The Catechism* notes that "the text before the asterisk (*) is from chap. 67." The ellipsis and parentheses are in the *Catechism*.

126 Joseph Fessenden, "The Roman Canon: Its History and Theology with a Brief Exegesis of the Institution Narrative," research paper for the course "History and Theology of the Liturgy," https://frjoe.com/wp-content/uploads/2014/10/SL-502-History-and-Theology-of-the-Roman-Canon.pdf.

127 Adrian Fortescue, "Canon of the Mass," *The Catholic Encyclopedia*. Vol. 3. (New York: Robert Appleton Company, 1908), http://www.newadvent.org/cathen/03255c.htm, accessed on April 17, 2024.

128 *Luther's Works*, Vol. 51: Sermons I. John H. Doberstein and Helmut T. Lehman, eds., (Philadelphia: Fortress Press, 1959), 75.

129 Martin Luther, *Smalcald Articles*, Article II: Of the Mass (1537), https://www.gutenberg.org/files/273/273-h/273-h.htm, accessed on April 17, 2024.

130 *The Table Talk of Martin Luther*, tr. William Hazlitt, Christian Classics Ethereal Library, originally published by The Lutheran Publication Society, Philadelphia, n.d., CLXXI, https://www.ccel.org/ccel/luther/tabletalk.html, accessed on April 17, 2024.

131 *What Luther Says: A Practical In-Home Anthology for the Active Christian*, compiled by Ewald M. Plass. (St. Louis: Concordia Publishing House, 1959), 793 (quote 2466), ellipsis in original. The original quote is from Weimar 38:266 f.

132 *Ibid.*, quote 2855, p. 912, brackets in original. The original quote is from Weimar 30 II, 293.

133 *Ibid.*, quote 2856, p. 913, parentheses in original. The original quote is from the *Table Talk* 2, No. 2495, Weimar edition.

134 Martin Luther, *On the Misuse of Mass* (German version), 1521, quoted in Grisar, 208.

135 *Ibid.*

136 *Dictata in Psalterium*. Weimar III, 445. Cf. also IV, 363; cited in Heinrich Denifle, *Luther and Lutherdom*, Vol. I, Part I, tr. Raymund Volz (Somerset, OH: Torch Press, 1917), 15.